Soho Theatre presents

ROLLER DINER

By Stephen Jackson

Roller Diner was first performed at Soho Theatre, London on Friday 26th May 2017.

Published by Playdead Press 2017

© Stephen Jackson 2017

Stephen Jackson has asserted his rights under the Copyright, Design and Patents Act, 1988, to be identified as the authors of this work.

A CIP catalogue record for this book is available from the British Library.

ISBN 978-1-910067-47-5

Playdead Press
www.playdeadpress.com

Soho Theatre presents

ROLLER DINER

By Stephen Jackson

CAST

Eddie	Joe Dixon
Mysterious Woman / Jean	Rina Fatania
Marika	Lucy McCormick
PJ	Ricky Oakley
Mysterious Man / Roger	David Thaxton
Chantal	Lucie Shorthouse

CREATIVE TEAM

Playwright and Composer	Stephen Jackson*
Director	Steve Marmion
Set and Costume Designer	Anthony Lamble
Lighting Designer	Philip Gladwell
Sound Designer	Mic Pool
Musical Director	David Thaxton
Musical Arranger	Stephen Edwards
Choreographer	Stuart Rogers
Costume Supervisor	Scarlet Wallis
Production Manager	Andreas Ayling
Assistant Director	Lakesha Arie Angelo
Casting Director	Nadine Rennie CDG
Fight Director	Bret Yount
Deputy Stage Manager	Ruthie Philip-Smith
Stage Manager	Stephanie Joab
Assistant Stage Manager	Claudia Bryan-Joyce

Death of a Dreamer co-written with Jane Cashmore

LONDON'S MOST VIBRANT
VENUE FOR NEW THEATRE,
COMEDY AND CABARET

Soho Theatre is a major creator of new theatre, comedy and cabaret. Across our three different spaces we curate the finest live performance we can discover, develop and nurture. Soho Theatre works with theatre makers and companies in a variety of ways, from full producing of new plays, to co-producing new work, working with associate artists and presenting the best new emerging theatre companies that we can find.

We have numerous writers and theatre makers on attachment and under commission, six young writers and comedy groups and we read and see hundreds of shows a year – all in an effort to bring our audience work that amazes, moves and inspires.

'Soho Theatre was buzzing, and there were queues all over the building as audiences waited to go into one or other of the venue's spaces. [The audience] is so young, exuberant and

clearly anticipating a good time.' Guardian

We attract over 170,000 audience members a year. We produced, co-produced or staged over forty new plays in the last twelve months.

Our social enterprise business model means that we maximise value from Arts Council and philanthropic funding; we actually contribute more to government in tax and NI than we receive in public funding.

sohotheatre.com

Keep up to date:
sohotheatre.com/mailing-list
facebook.com/sohotheatre
twitter.com/sohotheatre
youtube.com/sohotheatre

Registered Charity No: 267234

Soho Theatre, 21 Dean Street
London W1D 3NE
Admin 020 7287 5060
Box Office 020 7478 0100

LOTTERY FUNDED

Supported using public funding by
**ARTS COUNCIL
ENGLAND**

SUBMITTING YOUR WORK TO SOHO THEATRE

We make the very best entertaining, challenging, profound new work across a range of live performance genres.

We are the place where emerging and established writers conceive, develop and realise their work.

We want to push the form in a way that delights and inspires our audience.

There are no thematic, political or philosophical constraints and though we love to produce a writers' first play, we have no objection to your second, third or fiftieth.

We are looking for unique and unheard voices – from all backgrounds, attitudes and places.

We want to make things you've never seen before.

If you would like to submit a script to us please send it as a PDF or Word attachment to: **submissions@sohotheatre.com**

Your play will go directly to our Artistic team.

We consider every submission for production or for further development opportunities. Although there are a limited number of slots on our stages, we engage with writers throughout the year through workshops, readings, notes sessions and other opportunities.

Soho Theatre is a charity and social enterprise. We are supported by Arts Council England and we put every £1 donated back into our work. Our supporters are key to our success and we are immensely grateful for their support. We would like to thank all our supporters for their generosity:

van den Bossche
Ann Stanton
Alex Vogel
Sian and Matthew
Westerman
Mark Whiteley
Gary Wilder
Alexandra Williams
Hilary and Stuart
Williams

**Soho Theatre Dear
Friends**
Nick Allan
Christiane Amanpour
Ken Anderson
David Aukin
Natalie Bakova
James Boyle
Rajan Brotia
James Brown
Simon Brown, Founder
The ESTAS Group
Lisa Bryer
Steve Coogan
Fiona Dewar
Cherry and Rob Dickins
Manu Duggal
Chris Evans
Denzil and Renate
Fernandez
Dominic Flynn
Jonathan Glanz and
Manuela Raimondo
Alban Gordon
Kate Horton
Fawn James
John James
Dede Johnston
Shappi Khorsandi
Jeremy King
Lynne Kirwin
Michael Kunz
David and Linda
Lakhdhir
Anita and Brook Land
Jonathan Levy
Patrick Marber
Nick Mason and
Annette Lynton Mason
Aoife O'Brien
Adam Morley
Aoife O'Brien
Rick Pappas
Natasha Parker
Leanne Pollock

Lauren Prakke
Phil and Jane Radcliff
John Reid
James Robertson
Sue Robertson
Alexandra Sears
Robert & Melanie
Stoutzker
Dominic and Ali Wallis
Garry Watts
Gregg Wilson
Andrea Wong
Matt Woodford
Henry Wyndham
Christopher Yu

**Soho Theatre Good
Friends**
Oladipo Agboluaje
James Atkinson
Jonathan and Amanda
Baines
Uri Baruchin
Antonio Batista
Alex Bridport
Jesse Buckle
Indigo Carnie
Paul Carpenter
Chris Carter
Sharon Eva Degen
Michelle Dietz
Niki di Palma
Jeff Dormer
Geoffrey and Janet
Eagland
Edwina Ellis
Peter Fenwick
Gail and Michael Flesch
Sue Fletcher-
James Flitton
Cyrus Gilbert-Rolfe
Eva Greenspan
Doug Hawkins
Etan Ilfeld
John Ireland
Fran Jones
Eric Knopp
Susie Lea
Simon Lee
Tom Levi
Ian Livingston
Nicola Martin
Kathryn Marten
Amanda Mason
Neil Mastrarrigo

Robert McFarland
Gerry McGrail
Andrew and Jane
McManus
Mr and Mrs Roger
Myddelton
Dr Tara Naidoo
Max Nicholson
Alan Pardoe
Nick Pontt
Edward Pivcevic
Sadia Quyam
Stephanie Ressort
Barry Serjent
Ed Smith
Hari Sriskantha
Francis and Marie-
Claude Stobart
Sam Swallow
Lesley Symons
Sue Terry
Gabriel Vogt
Anja Weise
Mike Welsh
Matt Whitehurst
Allan Willis
Liz Young

We would also like to
thank those supporters
who wish to remain
anonymous.

Soho Theatre has the
support of the
Channel 4 Playwrights'
Scheme sponsored by
Channel 4 Television.

We are also supported
by Westminster City
Council West End
Ward Budget and the
London Borough of
Waltham Forest.

CAST

EDDIE | JOE DIXON

Joe Dixon is a Royal Shakespeare Company Associate Artist. His theatre credits include: *The Tempest, The Orphan of Zhao, Boris Godunov, A Midsummer Night's Dream, Love's Labours Lost, Titus Andronicus, The Malcontent, The Island Princess, The Roman Actor* and *The Comedy of Errors* (all RSC); *Cruel and Tender* (Young Vic); *As You Like It* (Cheek By Jowl); *The Duchess of Malfi* (Greenwich/Wyndhams); *Romeo & Juliet* (ESC); *The Bacchae* (QEH Southbank Centre); *Le Bourgeois Gentilhomme / Ariadne Auf Naxos* (Nottingham Playhouse / Scottish Opera / Festival Theatre Edinburgh); *A Winter's Tale* (National Theatre); *Women Beware Women* (Royal Court Theatre); *Our Country's Good* (Gate Theatre, Dublin). Film credits include: *The Cold Light of Day; 14 Days With Victor; The Mummy Returns; The Changeling; Rise of the Footsoldier.* Television credits include: *Doctor Who* (BBC); *Vera* (ITV); *The Coroner* (BBC); *A.D. The Bible Continues* (NBC) and *Atlantis* (BBC Wales).

MYSTERIOUS WOMAN/JEAN | RINA FATANIA

Rina Fatania's theatre Credits include: *Anita & Me* (UK Tour); *Sinbad the Sailor* (Theatre Royal Stratford East); *Paradise of the Assassins* (Tara Arts); *Love N Stuff* (Theatre Royal Stratford East); *Dead Dog in a Suitcase* (Kneehigh); *Mummyji Presents* (Birmingham Rep); *Aladdin* (De Montford Hall, Leicester); *The Empress* (RSC); *Dick Whittington* (Hackney Empire); *Wah! Wah! Girls* (Sadler's Wells); *Cinderella* (Hackney Empire); *Guantanamo Boy* (Brolly Productions); *Britain's Got Bhangra* (UK Tour); *The Vagina Monologues* (Alchemy Festival, Southbank); *The House of Bilquis Bibi* (Hampstead Theatre); *Britain's Got Bhangra, Meri Christmas, The Deranged Marriage* (Rifco Arts); *Wuthering Heights, A Fine Balance, The Child of Divide, Strictly Dandia* (Tamasha); *It Aint All Bollywood*

(Rifco Arts / UK & Pakistan tour); *Bombay Dreams* (Apollo Victoria); *Arabian Nights* (Midland Arts Centre). Film Credits include: *Raabta* (Bollywood Film); *Digital-Mummji Presents* (Character devised by Rina Fatania); *Mumbai Charlie* (Pukkanasha Films); *The Travel Londoner* (Painting Pictures). Radio Credits include: *Bindi Business*, *Baby Farming*, *We Are Water*, *Oceans Unite Us*, *Silver Street* (all BBC).

MARIKA | LUCY MCCORMICK
Lucy's debut solo show *Triple Threat* had a sell-out run at the 2016 Edinburgh Festival Fringe followed by a month long run at Soho Theatre. Lucy was nominated for Emerging Artist at the Total Theatre Awards and was the winner of the TV Bomb Groundbreaker Award. *Triple Threat* was included in the Guardian's Top Ten Comedy Shows of 2016. Lucy also co-founded GETINTHEBACKOFTHEVAN performance company in 2008 with whom she has performed extensively in both UK and Europe at venues including Soho Theatre, Almeida Theatre, Latitude Festival, Anti Festival (Finland), Festwochen (Vienna), PACT Zollverein (Germany), BoraBora (Denmark) and Noorderzon Festival (Netherlands). Further acting credits include *Cinderella* (Oxford Playhouse); *The Naked Truth* (National tour); *First Love is the Revolution* (Soho Theatre); *Splat!* (Barbican); *Dusa, Fish, Stas and Vi* (Northern Lights); *As You Like It* (Wirksworth Festival); *On Stage: Live From Television Centre* (BBC FOUR) and *Uncle David 2* (Avant-garde Film Alliance).

PJ | RICKY OAKLEY
Ricky Oakley trained at Rose Bruford. His theatre credits include: *King David* (Finborough Theatre); *The Comedy of Errors* (The Orange Tree); *Posh* (Barons Court Theatre); *Britain Ltd* (Theatre Ad Infinitum) and *Hamlet* (Shakespeare's Globe). Theatre credits whilst training: *The Low Road*, *Today*, *Pericles* and *The Trial*.

CHANTAL | LUCIE SHORTHOUSE

Lucie Shorthouse's theatre credits include: *Everybody's Talking About Jamie* (Sheffield Theatres); *The House of In Between* (Theatre Royal Stratford East); *The Comedy of Errors* (Sam Wanamaker Festival at Shakespeare's Globe). Her television credits include: *Line of Duty* (World Productions/BBC); *Doctors* (BBC) and *The Sound of Music Live* (ITV)

MYSTERIOUS MAN/ROGER | DAVID THAXTON

David Thaxton trained at the *Royal Welsh College of Music and Drama*. His theatre includes: *Jesus Christ Superstar* (Regent's Park Open Air Theatre); *Passion* (Donmar Warehouse, Olivier Award for Best Actor in a Musical); *Candide* (Menier Chocolate Factory); *Only The Brave*, *The Rake's Progress*, *The Tailor's Daughter* (all Wales Millennium Centre); *Les Misérables* (Queen's Theatre); *Love Never Dies* (Adelphi); *The Cunning Little Vixen* (Sherman Theatre). David is a founding member of Divisions, a 5-piece band from the UK who create thrilling, atmospheric and epic alternative rock. Their debut album, *Distance Over Time*, is out now.

CREATIVE TEAM

PLAYWRIGHT | STEPHEN JACKSON

Although Roller Diner is Stephen Jackson's first professional production, he has been scribbling away on the twilit fringes of the civilised theatre world... His first play Ouija! was shortlisted for the International Playwriting Festival - though never performed – and he has been shortlisted for the Keats-Shelley Prize for Poetry. He also doodled cartoons and greetings cards before illustrating his own children's optical illusion adventure book Mirrorworld. ("A fantastic idea and brilliantly produced - Mirrorworld is addictive." The Sunday Times.) Stephen is a member of BOLDtext – a collective of playwrights who stage regular scratch nights – and his comedy The Bingo Caller is about to get a final polish before it ends up on stage somewhere soon... He only started writing songs seriously for Roller Diner, but now he can't stop – even when begged. He has recently been supporting his artistic dreams by working as an inventory clerk.

DIRECTOR | STEVE MARMION

Steve Marmion is Artistic Director of Soho Theatre. Since joining Soho Theatre he has directed Bits of Me Are Falling Apart, First Love is the Revolution, Death of a Comedian (co-production with Lyric Belfast and Abbey Dublin), I Kiss Your Heart, The One, The Night Before Christmas, Address Unknown, Pastoral, The Boy Who Fell Into A Book, Utopia, Fit and Proper People, Mongrel Island and Realism. In March 2016 he directed the new musical Only the Brave (Wales Millennium Centre). Over the past two years he has written and directed the Oxford Playhouse pantos: Cinderella (2016) and Aladdin (2015) Prior to joining Soho Theatre, Steve directed Macbeth for Regent's Park Open Air Theatre and Dick Whittington, Aladdin and Jack and the Beanstalk for the Lyric Hammersmith. In 2009 he directed the highly successful

production of *Edward Gant's Amazing Feats of Loneliness*
for Headlong Theatre, which received rave reviews at
Soho Theatre. In 2008 he had three critically praised
successes with *Vincent River* in New York, the original
Edinburgh production of *Only the Brave* and *Metropolis*
in Bath. He also transferred Rupert Goold's *Macbeth* onto
Broadway. Steve was Assistant, then Associate Director,
at the RSC over two years from 2006-07. In 2004 he
directed several premieres for Sir Alan Ayckbourn at the
Stephen Joseph Theatre and returned to direct the
Christmas show in 2006. He has worked with the National
Theatre, RSC, in the West End, on Broadway, at the Royal
Court, Lyric Hammersmith, Theatre Royal Plymouth,
Theatre Royal Bath, Watford Palace Theatre, Sherman
Theatre Cardiff and Edinburgh Fringe Festival. *Only the
Brave* (2008) was nominated for Best New Musical and
Best New Music at the MTM: UK Awards, and his *Madam
Butterfly's Child* (2004) and *Mad Margaret's Revenge*
(2005) won the London One Act Theatre Festival.

SET AND COSTUME DESIGNER | ANTHONY LAMBLE
Anthony Lamble's theatre credits include: *First Love is the
Revolution* and *The One* (both Soho Theatre); *The Inn at
Lydda, Omeros, Romeo and Juliet* (all Shakespeare's
Globe); *Allegro, Three Sisters, Shivered* (all Southwark
Playhouse); *Baba ve Piç - The Bastard of Istanbul*
(Istanbul); *Pygmalion* (Vienna); *The Tempest* (RSC/Ohio);
Twitstorm, Dead Monkey (Park Theatre); *Richard III,
Clarion, Shrapnel, Ghost* from a Perfect Place (all Arcola);
The Devil Masters, Spoiling (also Stratford East), *Ciara*
(also Citizens' Theatre), *The Artist Man and the Mother
Woman, The Arthur Conan Doyle Appreciation Society*
(all Traverse Theatre); *Hamlet, Boa, Third Finger Left
Hand* (Trafalgar Studios); *Peter Pan* (Bloomsbury Theatre);
The Two Worlds of Charlie F (UK Tour/Toronto); *Shush,
The Passing, The East Pier, Bookworms, The Comedy of
Errors, The Playboy of the Western World* (all Dublin);
Relatively Speaking (Watermill); *The Price* (West

End/Tour); *Singer, Loot* (both Tricycle Theatre); *The Caucasian Chalk Circle, Translations, Sing Yer Heart Out for the Lads, A Midsummer Night's Dream, As You Like It* (all National Theatre); *The Tempest, Measure for Measure, Richard III, The Roman Actor, King Baby* (all RSC); *The Entertainer* (Old Vic); *The English Game* (Headlong); *The World's Biggest Diamond, Incomplete and Random Acts of Kindness, Mother Teresa is Dead, Herons* (all Royal Court); *The English Game* (Headlong / WYP). Anthony has also designed productions for Chichester Festival Theatre, Hampstead, Lyric Hammersmith, West Yorkshire Playhouse, Dundee Rep, Bush Theatre, Sheffield Crucible, ETT, Shared Experience, Coventry Belgrade, Theatre Royal Northampton and Leicester Haymarket. His dance and opera credits include productions for English National Ballet, English National Opera, Royal Opera House and Opera City Tokyo. His television and film credits include: *Citizen Khan, Hebburn* (BBC Media City); *The Secret Audience* (Jolyon Symonds Productions Ltd) and *Joe Lycett DVD* (Duchess Theatre).

LIGHTING DESIGNER | PHILIP GLADWELL
Philip Gladwell's theatre credits include: *The Boy Who Fell into A Book* and *Pastoral* (both Soho Theatre); *Blanc de Blanc* (Sydney Opera House/ Hippodrome London); *Cymbeline* (RSC); *Limbo Unhinged* (Adelaide Fringe Festival); *Limbo* (International Tour); *Magic Mike Live* (Las Vegas); *The James Plays* (National Theatre of Scotland & International Tour); *Hairspray* (UK & Asia tour); *A Midsummer Night's Dream* (Barbican & US tour); *Fraulein Julie* (Schaubuhne Berlin & Barbican); *Terminus* (Public Theatre NY); *Much Ado About Nothing* (Shakespeare's Globe); *Milk, Swallow, Ciara* (all Traverse Theatre Scotland); *The World of Extreme Happiness, Love the Sinner* (both National Theatre); *Five Guys Named Moe* (Underbelly); *Jackie the Musical* (UK Tour); *Mr. Burns, Before The Party* (both Almeida); *The Seagull* (Regent's Park); *The Member of the Wedding* (Young Vic); *The*

Twits, Liberian Girl, God Bless The Child, The Ritual Slaughter of Gorge Mastromas, No Quarter (all Royal Court).

SOUND DESIGNER | MIC POOL

Mic Pool's West End and Broadway credits include: *Art* (worldwide); *Brand, Breakfast at Tiffany's* (Haymarket); *The King's Speech* (Wyndham's); *The Postman Always Rings Twice* (Playhouse); *The Madness of George III* (Apollo); *The Unexpected Man, The Hound of the Baskervilles* (Duchess); *When We Are Married* (Savoy); *Dr Faustus* (Fortune); *The 39 Steps* (Tony Award winner for Best Sound). Other sound designs include: *Dial M for Murder, Abigail's Party* (national tours); *The Captain of Kopenick* (National Theatre); *A Midsummer Night's Dream, The Seagull, The Roundhouse Season of Late Shakespeare Plays* (all RSC); *No's Knife, Fortune's Fool* (both Old Vic); *The Night Before Christmas* (Soho); *Gaslight* (Royal Northampton); *Beryl, Single Spies* (both Rose Kingston); *The Stopping Train, Overworlds and Underworlds* (Gavin Bryars); *Our Country's Good* (Out of Joint); *The Graduate* (West Yorkshire Playhouse); *Touched, Faith Healer* (Royal Court); *The Ice Chimney, Summer with Monika* (Lyric Hammersmith); *Shockheaded Peter* and Rambert Dance Company (world tours).

MUSICAL ARRANGER | STEPHEN EDWARDS

Stephen Edwards has produced over 50 productions and directed *Master Class, Amadeus, Sweeney Todd, A Christmas Carol, Animal Farm, Frankenstein, Oh! What Lovely War!, My Dad's Corner Shop* and *Johnno* for the Brisbane Festival. Stephen was nominated for a TMA Award for *Moon Landing*, which is being remounted in Germany and the USA to coincide with 50th Anniversary of the 1st Lunar Landing. As a composer his work includes: *4 Baboons Adoring The Sun* in collaboration with John Guare, Lincoln Centre (New York) which was nominated for 3 Tony Awards; *Trackers Of Oxyrhynchus* in collaboration with Tony Harrison at the National Theatre (London) which was nominated for 3 Olivier Awards; and a long association with Peter Hall at the National Theatre and his company in London and New York.

CHOREOGRAPHER | STUART ROGERS

Stuart Rogers' choreography credits include: *A Teenage Opera* (NYT); *Club Mexicano* (New Musical Workshop); *Bare* (Old Finsbury Town Hall); *Cinderella* (Oxford Playhouse); *Cinderella* (Harlequin Theatre). He was Creative Director for The Stylophones album launch at the Leicester Square Theatre and The Stylophones *Confidential Encounters* music video. Assistant choreography credits include: *Strictly Come Dancing* plus many corporate and TV events. His performing credits include: *Oh! What A Night!* (UK tour); Matthew Bourne's *Nutcracker* (Sadlers Wells and Japan/Korea tour); *Fame the musical* (West end, Mary Poppins west end, Mamma Mia west end, Sinatra UK tour, Footloose UK tour, Never Forget UK tour, We Will Rock You West end, The Bodyguard West end. Dancer for Emma Bunton's "Maybe" video and the following TV campaign.

ASSISTANT DIRECTOR | LAKESHA ARIE-ANGELO

Lakesha is Soho Theatre's Resident Director. Previous directing includes: *AS:NT* (Theatre 503) as part of Rapid Write; *Prodigal* (Bush Theatre) for 'Artistic Directors of the Future Black Lives: Black Words'. Scratch of *Sugar, Rum, Molasses* (CLF Theatre) as writer and director. As Resident Assistant Director at Finborough Theatre: *P'Yongyang*, *Treasure* and the Vibrant 2015 Festival of Finborough Playwrights. During the residency, Lakesha was awarded the Richard Carne Trust sponsorship.

Roller Diner is dedicated to Jean Wilde, Marcus Hendry, Lucy Poulson, Matt Ludlam, Rachael Louise Pickard, David Edgar (aka Mike Nicholas), Christine Bland, Geddes Cureton and Heather Matuozzo – an unforgettable team!

EDDIE COSTELLO
50, owner of the Roller Diner.

CHANTAL
19, his daughter, Roller Diner waitress.

PJ
19, her boyfriend and the chef.

MARIKA
early 20s, an East European waitress.

MYSTERIOUS WOMAN
40s, a female customer, East European accent.

MYSTERIOUS MAN
40s, a male customer, East European accent.

JEAN
50, an Asian Brummie waitress.

ROGER
50, a customer.

JEAN and MYSTERIOUS WOMAN are played by the same actor.

ROGER and MYSTERIOUS MAN are played by the same actor.

Please note that the text of the play which appears in this volume may be changed during the rehearsal process and appear in a slightly altered form in performance.

Roller Diner

Act 1

Eddie Costello's dilapidated Roller Diner. Monday morning.

A short counter - placed centrally at the back of the stage - is square on to the audience. This is where the flipping and frying takes place. The staff can walk round it either way. A doorway behind it is covered with a beaded curtain. Stage right is the exit to the shop door – and stage left is the exit to upstairs and the backyard – which we never see.

MYSTERIOUS MAN sits at a table at the right front corner of the stage – and MYSTERIOUS WOMAN, sits at a table at the front left corner of the stage. Both are motionless, staring out towards the audience. They mirror each other. They are East Europeans and dressed quite severely. And of course they add dispassionate backing vocals and harmonies when required.

EDDIE, 50, is opening the Roller Diner. He's scruffy – a grubby white overall coat.

RADIO   Rain, rain, rain, rain, rain... but a heatwave on the way... by the end of the week - that's what the weatherman says so keep your umbrella handy and let's celebrate with a slow sad, slow sad classic...

                (*sings*) *Before you*
                Polish my boots
                And bury me
                In my blue suit
                Beneath the cherry trees

RADIO /   *(joins in) Please brush my hair to one side*
EDDIE   *But don't cry*
                      Don't cry
                      For I am a man who'll die
                      With no tears left burning inside
                      It's just my time
                      My time
                      My time

Eddie vanishes. Lights up

PJ is the chef. He's a boyish 19. He wears the chef's check trousers but not the hat.

PJ   *(to audience)* It was Monday morning. Me
                      and Chantal were just larking around.
                      (sings) How I miss your candy kisses babe
                      How I wish the memory would never fade...
                      away
                      Tell me how you need me
                      Don't walk away
                      Never leave me
                      How I miss your candy kisses babe

Enter CHANTAL, 19, waitress and PJ's girlfriend. She wears the Roller Diner uniform. She has pink hair and chews gum.

CHANTAL   I'm only here.

PJ   That's too far.

CHANTAL   I've gotta get the burgers from out the
                      back.

PJ   That's too far away... It hurts.

CHANTAL   How far can I go then...? *(She backs away)*

PJ   That's too far!

CHANTAL   Oh, PJ, you are a prat.

PJ   Chantal...

CHANTAL   Tell me again...

PJ   Tell you what?

CHANTAL   *Tell me how you need me*

PJ   *Don't walk away*

CHANTAL   *Never leave me*

TOGETHER   *How I miss your candy kisses, babe*

They share a pouty kiss... MARIKA has appeared unnoticed during this song. She wears a coat and has a tattered suitcase, roller skates tied on.

PJ   (*to audience*) Chantal and I were so busy messing about, I didn't even notice her come in.

M.MAN/M.WOMAN (*sinister whisper*)   Ma-ri-ka!!

CHANTAL   (*to audience*) I didn't even smell her – and I can smell trouble.

PJ   (*to audience*) Probably cos of them sausages I burnt... She just walked in off the street.

CHANTAL   (*to audience*) Out of the blue

PJ   (*to audience*) Out of the rain actually...

CHANTAL   (*to audience*) She was full of it.

21

MARIKA   You are the chef... I can tell by the silly
trousers

PJ   (*to audience*) She looked like a waif.

CHANTAL   (*to audience*) A stray.

M.MAN/M.WOMAN   (*sing*)   *A runaway*

PJ   (*to audience*) But she didn't strike me as
                the sort of girl who could provoke murder.

CHANTAL   (*to audience*) But she was the sort I could
                murder. Two or three times.

MARIKA   My name is Marika Malinski. Super duper
                waitress, I've come from Poland for the
                job. I'd look good in the sexy skirt - when
                I'm cleaning the ketchup from the tables.

CHANTAL   Just ketchup?

PJ   (*to audience*) We didn't even have a
                vacancy...

CHANTAL   (*to audience*) Especially not for looking
                sexy in the skirt... Position taken,
                darling...

MARIKA   I speak good English -

PJ   We only speak American here. That's
                supposed to be the rule.

MARIKA   I speak good American.

PJ   You'll have to speak it to Eddie, the boss —

CHANTAL   but he would've told me if we had a
                vacancy. In fact I would have told him.

MARIKA   I speak it to Eddie.

CHANTAL   *Mister* Costello. And I have to approve all the appointments.

MARIKA   Mister Costello.

EDDIE   (*American accent*) Who's asking?

EDDIE enters. PJ scuttles off back behind the counter to look busy.

EDDIE   (*Brummie accent from now on. To audience*) I'd just woken up. And I wasn't in a good mood.

PJ   (*to audience*) Never was. Eighteen stone of misery with ingrowing toenails.

EDDIE   (*reminding PJ*) And acid indigestion.

MARIKA   My name is Marika Malinski. (*She holds out her hand*)

CHANTAL   "Superduper waitress."

EDDIE   (*to audience*) It gives me wind.

MARIKA   I've come from Poland for the job. I work hard, I start early, I work late,

CHANTAL   She'd look very good in the sexy skirt.

EDDIE   (*indifferent*) Oh yes...

MARIKA   When I'm cleaning ketchup from the tables.

EDDIE   There's more to it than that, love.

CHANTAL   Mustard, brown sauce...

23

EDDIE	Anyway, it won't work on me. I ain't too impressed with women. I don't like employing them.
MARIKA	She's a woman.
EDDIE	She is not. That's my daughter. A different sort of animal altogether. It's women I don't like.
PJ	That is half the human population.
EDDIE	No, it's all the human population, PJ – because I don't like men neither, especially when they are poking their noses into high level management decisions. (directly to MARIKA) And I don't need anybody at the moment.
MARIKA	But I've brought my roller skates
EDDIE	Haha - no-one here can skate. You'll make the rest of us look bad.
CHANTAL	(to audience) I shouldn't have taken the piss. I suppose she was desperate.
MARIKA	I've come a long way.
EDDIE	On those? (He's looking at the roller skates). You must be plum tuckered, love.
MARIKA	Don't laugh at me, Mr Eddie Costello.

Silence.

PJ	(to audience) No-one messed with Eddie. He might be a bit fat but it wasn't that soft fat –

EDDIE   (*to audience*) Hard fat.

PJ   (*to audience*) More like gristle

EDDIE   (*to audience*) plus me bad effin temper. But she looks me in the eye -

MARIKA   I could walk out of the door and make my fortune anywhere. I could pick fruit, or do something glamorous like hotel receptionist – but you're lucky that I'm in the middle of this pouring raining city and I see... Eddie Costello's Roller Diner – a little bit of the America dream here in dirty Birmingham, the lights shining in the pavement. Of course, inside it's disappointing. Greasy. Dingy. The windows are steamed up. The staff are, well... (*they all lean in...*)

CHANTAL   What?

MARIKA   Incompetent

EDDIE   Ha–ha. That's what I keep telling them.

CHANTAL   Gobby cow.

MARIKA   inefficient, inexperienced -

M.WOMAN / M.MAN   in love.

EDDIE   (*to audience*) I was starting to like this girl.

MARIKA   (*to EDDIE*) and you look like you come to work straight from your coffin.

EDDIE   (*to audience*) Maybe not.

MARIKA   But that's why you need me...

25

EDDIE   I'm sure you're right, darling, but we don't
             have a job, do we, Chantal?

CHANTAL   Already told her.

MARIKA   Hang on, Mr Business Brains Costello.
             You haven't heard the deal yet. And I'm
             sure you were a business man once before
             your heart got broken...

EDDIE   Who told you that?

MARIKA   Smell this place... (*they all sniff*) you can
             smell the failure, you can smell the broken
             dreams... (*they all sniff*)

PJ   No, I think it's just them sausages...

EDDIE   (*to audience*) And I am still a businessman.

PJ   (*still sniffing*) Does tend to linger.

MARIKA   So here's my offer: I work for 2 weeks. I
             clean this place up. I teach him to cook,
             her to wipe the tables. Maybe I even I
             teach you how to be a boss — all for
             nothing. Free of charge. After 2 weeks,
             when you all like and love me - you'll give
             me a proper job - probably manageress.

PJ   (*to audience*) A blind man in sunglasses
             could see this was trouble.

CHANTAL   (*to audience*) And if he couldn't see it, his
             labrador would whisper in his ear

ALL   (*whisper*) Trouble.

EDDIE	(*to audience*) On the other hand...Chantal and PJ were off on holiday on Friday.
PJ	(*grinning to audience, thumbs up*) Tenerife!!
CHANTAL	Only going for 5 days.
PJ	(*to audience*) We'd had it booked for ages. Sun, sea, sand, sangria -
M.WOMAN	Sex.
EDDIE	(*to audience*) So she could come in very useful.
MARIKA	That's a deal then.
CHANTAL	Dad?
EDDIE	(*to MARIKA*) For nothing?
MARIKA	Nothing. Except... I eat as much as I want.
EDDIE	(*to audience*) She wasn't too fat...
CHANTAL	That's because she's starving...
EDDIE	(*to audience*) No-one could eat much of PJ's cooking.
PJ	(*laughs, stops*) Hang on -
EDDIE	(*to audience*) You've got to give people a chance haven't you?
CHANTAL	Especially the pretty ones.
MARIKA	Good. I start now.
CHANTAL	Dad?

27

EDDIE   And specially when they'll graft for
               nothing. Chantal - find the girl a uniform.

CHANTAL   No way.

EDDIE   Any nonsense, I ring the authorities – any
               stealing, I chop your hands off. And don't
               bring your hairy grandmother and her
               goat round here and think I'm gonna feed
               em. I'm not a sympathetic person. PJ you
               do the money - no foreign fingers in the
               till. This isn't a charity...

MARIKA   I understand - no grandmothers, no goats.

EDDIE   And don't you forget, Machinka, who's the
               big soft hearted fellah who's giving you a
               chance.

MARIKA   I never forget. (*To PJ*) Ok, chef, I'll have
               the veggie burger, fried tomatoes, the
               baked beans, the chips and... the ice-
               cream.

CHANTAL   She hasn't done any work yet.

MARIKA   Stand still, Mr Eddie Costello, and close
               your eyes. Both of them. (*He closes his eyes
               and she gives him a kiss on the cheek.*) You
               are going to give me a job in two weeks
               time... probably manageress. You'll be
               begging me to stay. You'll give me as
               much ice-cream as I want. You see. You'll
               want to cover me in it.

CHANTAL   What did she just say?

M.WOMAN   Sex -

28

M.MAN	the world's biggest export
M.WOMAN	from the poor
M.MAN	to the rich.
EDDIE	Chantal? Where's the uniform?

CHANTAL folds her arms. The Mopping Song starts. MARIKA takes off her coat and hangs it on Chantal. MARIKA is already wearing the uniform... Montage of change underscored by The Mopping Song as the staff mop, clean and criss-cross the stage during the following dialogue....

EDDIE	(*to audience*) In two weeks time I can guarantee she wasn't going to be manageress here, Mar...
MARIKA	Marika Malinski! Superduper hardworking waitress.
EDDIE	(*to audience*) In two weeks time, she was going to be Prime Minister...
CHANTAL	(*to audience*) Or murdered.
EDDIE	(*to audience*) I didn't know how much trouble she'd bring.
PJ	(*to audience*) A grafter, though.
MARIKA	Erghh... (*she has picked up a bottle of ketchup*)
EDDIE	(*to audience*) A proper grafter.
MARIKA	This ketchup is all sticky...

CHANTAL	It's meant to be sticky. It's traditional. (*To audience*) And she didn't look *that* good in the skirt.
MARIKA	It's these uniforms. We need new uniforms. Who chose these terrible things?
CHANTAL	I did.
EDDIE	Big impact...
CHANTAL	(*to audience*) on some more than others... (*PJ is looking at MARIKA*)
PJ	What? What?
EDDIE	(*to audience*) You couldn't find out much about her. If you asked her a question -
MARIKA	It doesn't matter where somebody is from - it's where they are going that counts.
EDDIE	(*to audience*) She'd answer in riddles. Yet somehow she seemed to find out about everybody else.
MARIKA	It isn't your wife that's run away, Eddie, it's you. Run away from life.
CHANTAL	(*to audience*) What business is that of hers? My mother?

PJ gently restrains her.

MARIKA	Run away from life and quietly died.
CHANTAL	(*to audience*) PJ Blabbermouth – would tell her anything.
PJ	I haven't said a word.

30

MARIKA	It's nothing personal, Eddie. Most people are like you – dead.
EDDIE	They look alive to me.
MARIKA	Ghosts. Look out there – millions of them (*she indicates the audience*): ghosts of the people they could have been.
EDDIE	(*to audience*) Take no notice. I never understood what she was going on about either.
MARIKA	Your problem Eddie is that you've forgotten the future.

The music fades out as MARIKA exits.

CHANTAL	(*mimics*) "Who designed the menus?" (*points sarcastically at herself*)
EDDIE	(*to audience*) Ghost of the person I could have been?
CHANTAL	(*mimics*) "Who thought pink would look good in the toilets?" (*points sarcastically at herself*)
EDDIE	(*to audience*) Forgotten the future? It hasn't even happened yet.
CHANTAL	(*to audience*) He'd let a whirlwind loose in the Roller Diner.
PJ	(*to audience*) We'd been happy until then.

CHANTAL/ EDDIE   No, we hadn't.

Lights fade down except for dramatic lighting on M.WOMAN.

31

M.WOMAN	(*to audience*) *I remember the future*
	When it was morning
	Mist clearing from the peach trees
	And I ran towards it
	My hair streaming
	Now I want to stop, go back
M.MAN	(*sings*) *Oh woe woe* (*the 3 long notes from The Mopping Song*)
M.WOMAN	*But every way I turn*
M.MAN	(*sings*) *Oh woe woe*
M.WOMAN	*The future pours over the horizon*
	And floods through the black hills
	Towards me.
M.MAN/ M.WOMAN	(*sing*) *Oh woe woe... woe....* – (*into darkness - lights up*)
PJ	(*to audience*) Marika'd been there a couple of days... she's already bossing me about. And Chantal was not happy -
CHANTAL	(*fizzing across the back of the stage*) She doesn't come from Poland.
PJ	(*to audience*) People think Chantal is a bit of a cow – and she is - but on our own she can do funny walks and cartoon voices. She does a wicked Lisa off *The Simpsons*. Cracks me up. Truth is...
CHANTAL	(*fizzing across the front of the stage*) I think she's been spying on us.
PJ	(*sings*) *I sell my labour*

Don't talk a lot
Don't like the weather
When it's too hot

All I want's a quiet life
And this warm woman
For my -

CHANTAL   How come she piggin effin blindin cowing knows everything about us?

PJ   (*to audience*) *All I want's a quiet life*
           And this warm woman -

CHANTAL   I know you keep blabbing to her.

PJ   I don't.

M.WOMAN   Jealousy. That's a killer.

M.MAN   *My woman,*

M.WOMAN   *Maybe she lies curled*
           Beneath this dome of stars

M.MAN   *Behind the back of a fat merchant*
           Who shoots monkeys.

CHANTAL   Something's wrong... It's all wrong. She hasn't turned up here by accident. She knows stuff about us all...

Exit CHANTAL. Lights up on M.MAN

M.MAN   *I still dream of her –*
           The bitch, the whore, the witch
           Naked on the mountain tops

> *Howling for hairy men*
> *And my red heart weeps blood,*
> *It floods the valleys you doublecross.*

(MYSTERIOUS MAN and MYSTERIOUS WOMAN stand up simultaneously. He howls like a werewolf.)

> *Hear my breath,*
> *Hear my paws,*

M.WOMAN   *(sings) Oh woe woe*

M.MAN   *My heart drips green from the leaves of envy–*

M.WOMAN   *(sings) Oh woe woe*

M.MAN   *My brothers are grim,*
                    My hands are hairy

Both MYSTERIOUS MAN and MYSTERIOUS WOMAN turn and exit on their own sides of the stage. But just before she exits the MYSTERIOUS WOMAN stops and turns to the audience.

M.WOMAN   There are twisted dark places in this world

PJ   Ten-er-ife!!!

Lights up on PJ.

> *(to audience)* That's where I'm going to propose... I've bought the ring! I keep checking it 10 times a day. Sun, sea, sand, sangria... sex. Oh yes, it's guaranteed. It's in the brochure. Pages 2 to 17 – sex. Pages 19 to 31 – sex. Page 18 is a comparison chart about different hotel features – but the rest is just catching beach balls in skimpy swimwear, a big smile on your

34

face. That's what Chantal needs... Tenerife – places and things just absorb into us. Sometimes... the world is... stunning! I've just drunk some tea. It comes from Darjeeling and now it's inside me, dissolving into me. It's come across mountains and seas – and now it's inside me – stunning! All the way from Turkey...

(*sings*) *Gas in my car*
Money in my pockets
Above me the stars
Visited by rockets

ALL   *Shine on*
             Shine on

PJ   *Me*

ALL   *Shine on*
             Shine on

PJ   *Me*

             Oh Stunning world

ALL   *Stunning, stunning world*

PJ   *You're in my head, and in my heart, and my heart's in flames*

ALL   *Oh Stunning world*
             Stunning, stunning -

MARIKA pops up from behind the counter.

MARIKA   I've found it!

MARIKA pops down.

35

I knew it was here – da -dah!!! Your hat.

She's holding a chef's hat.

PJ   I've had enough comments about the silly trousers, thank you.

MARIKA   The trousers only look silly because you don't wear the hat like a proper chef.

PJ   I'm only flipping burgers.

MARIKA   That's why you should wear the hat. Look important like – the Pope! Nobody tells him he's wearing a silly hat.

PJ   They would if he worked here... frying the sausages. What if my mates come in – like Toe-Jam?

MARIKA   They'll love it. Everybody wants to know a great chef.

MARIKA has retrieved a cardboard box from under the counter.

                   Who's that? (*She pulls a framed photograph out of the box*)

PJ   Christ! (*snatches it off her*) That's Chantal's mum. Eddie's wife – his ex, the one that ran away. You know how to let Pandora out of the box, don't you?

MARIKA   Oh, that's her name.

PJ   We all say that – letting Pandora out of the box... hey!

36

Before PJ can put the picture back, he has noticed that MARIKA has opened the till.

What you doing?

MARIKA   I've seen how you open it.

PJ   Yeah, but what are you doing?

MARIKA   Stealing money.

MARIKA has taken some money and she closes the till.

PJ   (*to audience*) No way! Eddie will kill her. And me! Chrissake, Marika. Put it back. Come on!

PJ tries to grab the money. Enter CHANTAL. She is dressed in civvies and swamped by carrier bags from Next, Primark, Matalan, etc...

CHANTAL   Having fun, are we?

PJ   Nothing.

CHANTAL   What you doing?

MARIKA   Just playing. Happily.

MARIKA picks up the box and exits. PJ is a long way from the photograph at the other end of the counter.

PJ   (*To CHANTAL*) Did you get your new bikini?

CHANTAL   Hardly got anything.

(*she lets the mountain of bags fall, sits down and sings but PJ can't hear the song*)

It's a pretty day
But I don't know why
I'm
Moody

The cast pop up to sing "She's moody" but PJ interrupts –

PJ   What about them flip flops you wanted?

CHANTAL   Jelly flops.

The cast drop down embarrassed.

CHANTAL   (*sings*) *Checking out clothes*
              Choosin shoes
              Nothing I'd rather do
              But I'm moody

ALL   (*pop up*) *She's moody*
              Moody with you (*and down*)

CHANTAL   *Eaten alive*
              Suspicion on my mind
              And I'm moody

ALL   (*pop up*) *She's moody*
              Moody with you (*and down*)

PJ drops the chef's hat over the photograph just as CHANTAL turns round.

PJ   (*babbling*) I was going to ask you to get me
              another recipe book. Marika's going to
              show me how to make carrot dips... And
              puff pastry.

CHANTAL   Right...

PJ   Cup of tea?

38

CHANTAL	(*shakes her head*) Puff pastry?
PJ	What's wrong with that? For sausage rolls... And stuff.
CHANTAL	Nothing − not if it's for sausage rolls... And stuff. You just look a bit guilty that's all.
PJ	I don't.
CHANTAL	What's that then?
PJ	A hat. A chef's hat.

CHANTAL moves the hat and picks up the photograph.

CHANTAL	That's my mother. Why are you showing her pictures of my mother?
PJ	I'm not.
CHANTAL	Looks like my mother - same hair, same eyes...
PJ	No, yes it is. I mean Marika was helping your dad clean out the back.
CHANTAL	What?
PJ	I dunno. He was telling her all his old plans to knock it through − and the next thing they are clearing out boxes...
CHANTAL	He hasn't been out the back in 10 years.
PJ	Don't ask me. I'm just saying it wasn't me who was showing her pictures of your mom... OK?

CHANTAL   OK...

But CHANTAL calmly raises the photograph above her head and then shatters it on the floor.

> Puff... Fucking... Pastry.

She exits.

PJ   Chantal? Chantal?

PJ follows her off... Lights are lower. MARIKA alone on stage sweeping up the broken photograph with a dustpan and brush. Her coat is thrown over a chair. She is talking to someone but we don't know who.

MARIKA   (*matter of factly*) I said I'd look sexy in the skirt... when I was cleaning up.

Enter EDDIE, holding a glass. He's had a slight drink.

EDDIE   (*to audience*) Just checking she was doing the job properly. That's all.

MARIKA   You don't have to be embarrassed... though I heard that since your wife ran off you'd lost interest in women. Maybe you are not as dead as you look, dead Eddie – I thought you were as dead as your dog.

EDDIE   Who told you about my dog? (*to audience*) PJ, wasn't it? The arsehole of discretion.

MARIKA   Dead with your heart shrivelled up like a little mouse, tied on by its tail. Because a woman left him.

EDDIE   (*to audience*) My wife was everything to me...

He turns towards MARIKA starting to stretch out his arms. It's hard to tell whether this is the gesture of a lonely man or a sexual advance.

> You remind me of her.

MARIKA   I bet I do... because now you are ready for a woman again?

EDDIE   Well...

MARIKA has interpreted it as an advance and she's furious.

MARIKA   Her thin smooth limbs in your bed every night? Where I come from there are thousands of girls like me who love Englishmen. They think you were a millionaire. So grateful they make love three times a night - including once upside down and back to front.

EDDIE   Which part of Poland is this?

MARIKA   The part where they all dream of meeting sweaty Englishmen. Most of them have trained for years as acrobats for that very moment. Hunger does that to you – not just hunger for food, hunger for clothes, and shoes... Hunger means you can eat anything... rotten rancid vile.

EDDIE   What you mad at me for?

MARIKA   Hunger makes you lose your sense of taste, it makes you lose your sense of smell – you can swallow anything, it means you can eat fat sweaty Englishmen...

41

EDDIE	There's a misunderstanding -
MARIKA	So hungry you can sometimes eat two at a time...
EDDIE	I'm not into that kinky stuff -
MARIKA	You think women like me are cheap but if you want to fuck a woman like me, Eddie, you can't – you can't afford it.
EDDIE	I never even -
MARIKA	And if you want a wife like me, Eddie, do you know what it would cost?

MARIKA presses the photograph into EDDIE's hand.

EDDIE	How much?
MARIKA	(*pause*) Stand still, Mr Eddie Costello, and close your eyes. (*He closes his eyes and she gives him a kiss on the cheek.*) Get another dog. It's cheaper.

MARIKA goes to leave the cafe.

Or keep weeping for Pandora.

MARIKA exits.

EDDIE	(*to audience*) Who the fuck's Pandora? Come on, admit it... not even you women understand that girl, and you all communicate bloody telepathically.

EDDIE stares at the photograph of his wife and groans. He starts to rip the photograph in half, but can't do it. He goes to exit. PJ enters from the other side to collect Chantal's shopping bags.

PJ	Oh, Eddie... I need to have a word... about Marika –
EDDIE	Tomorrow.
PJ	It's about the money –
EDDIE	Tomorrow! ...Did you tell her about my dog?
PJ	What dog?

EDDIE exits.

(*to audience*) Oh, the *dog*. Before my time – but, apparently, when Eddie's dog died he cried every day for a year. I never mentioned it to Marika though. Don't even know if she likes dogs.

Enter CHANTAL in her dressing gown.

Are you checking up on me?

CHANTAL	Noh. (*to audience*) I bloody well was.
PJ	(*voice off*) Are you coming then?
CHANTAL	Might... (*to audience*) Got me radar on – and me laser night vision activated

CHANTAL takes off her dressing gown. She's wearing her uniform... The lights come up. She sits with her feet up.

I'm going to catch that girl with her fingers in the till – or her snout in the sausages - or her face in the trousers. Got me wing mirrors adjusted.

JEAN is wearing her coat. She marches in and stops dead. Then looks around amazed. She doesn't see CHANTAL. Enter MARIKA.

MARIKA   This morning we are offering all our customers free of charge the chance to try some carrot sticks and dips.

JEAN   Fuck me... Has Eddie died?

MARIKA   Of course not...

JEAN   Well, something's different. (*She picks up a bottle*) That ketchup should be sticky.

MARIKA   We have stopped the traditional ketchup.

JEAN   Have *we*? (*to audience*) I had a dream like this once... where everything was just a little bit different. So if I suddenly vanish, it means my alarm clock's gone off.

MARIKA   Would you prefer a carrot or a celery stick?

JEAN   I'm not a customer, love. I'm Jean. I work here.

She takes off her coat and hangs it on MARIKA. JEAN is wearing her uniform. During the following she removes her shoes and puts them on the table as she pulls on an enormous pair of slippers.

And I don't touch carrots unless they've been boiled for at least an hour. I'm very suspicious of vegetables.

MARIKA   I haven't heard of you.

JEAN   I haven't heard of you neither – and I've
                      been working here 20 years. (*Shouts*)

                      Alright PJ?

PJ   (*offstage*) Alright Jean.

MARIKA disdainfully carries away Jean's coat and shoes.

CHANTAL   (*to JEAN*) She reckons she looks sexy in
                      the skirt.

JEAN   Does she now? Well, I hope you told her –
                      position taken, darling.

She sashays towards the counter. Enter EDDIE.

                      (*flirty*) Alright, Eddie. (*She rolls her eyes
                      when he doesn't notice her.*)

EDDIE   (*to Chantal*) What are you doing? On
                      strike?

CHANTAL   I just thought we looked a bit overstaffed.
                      Thought I'd do something intelligent like
                      work out the stock situation so you know
                      what to order while we're away.

EDDIE   I think Marika's already done that. (*calls*)
                      PJ!

EDDIE goes to the counter. PJ enters.

                      When you've got a minute, show Marika
                      how to use the till.

PJ / CHANTAL   You what?

EDDIE   Well, while you two are sunning yourself
                      on some beach somewhere, Marika and

45

me, we'll be sweating our cobs off in here, won't we?

PJ   I thought you'd be doing the till.

EDDIE   (*to MARIKA*) Do you think you'll be able to handle it?

MARIKA   It looks complicated. But PJ, he's a good teacher.

CHANTAL   (*to audience*) Oh, PJ – brains of bleeding Britain.

PJ   I need to have a word.

EDDIE   Later. All right, Rog?

Enter ROGER – his eyes fixed on JEAN until she notices.

JEAN   (*to MARIKA*) You serve him. He's always leching over me.

EDDIE   (*to audience*) I liked Rog.

ROGER   (*to audience*) I liked Eddie.

EDDIE   (*to audience*) You could talk about things with him.

ROGER   (*to audience*) In depth.

EDDIE   Man to man.

ROGER   3-0

EDDIE   Offside

ROGER   Turbo.

EDDIE   4 be 2.

ROGER/EDDIE   Tits... (*to audience*) Top bloke.

Roger heads for a table.

JEAN   Leching, ogling, craving, lusting for me.

As MARIKA heads for Roger's table, CHANTAL comes alongside for a word.

CHANTAL   Thing is... with PJ - he's had a sheltered life. It's not your fault. He probably can't cope with lots of new ideas – all in a rush...

MARIKA   Like what?

CHANTAL   I don't know... ... ... puff pastry.

MARIKA   Pah! I don't want PJ.

CHANTAL   I didn't say you did... What's wrong with him?

MARIKA   Nothing – I just don't want a boy like PJ.

CHANTAL   Oh he's not good enough for you...   I suppose you only want superduper men?

MARIKA   Yes... superduper men (*she comes to the front of the stage and sings*)

        Why doncha rip my dress?
        Write "bitch" on me in my lipstick?
        Take me away, make my heart black
        Let me taste the rain rain
        Rain rain
        Rain rain
        Rain on your back

Why doncha tie my wrists
Burn me with your cigarette?
I wanna be shocking,
Blue with you
wanna wear black stockings, red red shoes…

(softly…) I wanna know how it feels
Passing through cities in your automobile
Wanna live sleazy
Wanna live low
On high heels in a cheap motel Oh -

JEAN   Psychosexual problems.

EDDIE   Don't swear at me.

JEAN   Your new waitress: haven't you noticed
              how she excites the men?

ROGER giggles as MARIKA takes his order… flirtatiously.

EDDIE   Can't say I've paid any attention.

JEAN   She's a tease. She'll show them her
              knickers but she won't take them off.

EDDIE   Better than nothing I suppose.

JEAN   No, Eddie – it's the behaviour of girls
              who've been damaged… abused. For them
              sex is loveless. It's a tool or a weapon. I
              know all about it

EDDIE   (*astonished*) Do you?

JEAN   Yes, I do. Big article in The *Cosmopolitan*.

PJ   (*explaining to MARIKA*) Always used to
              open evenings – didn't you, Jean?

48

JEAN   Till the Kelly Crew fight.

Tables turned over violently. ROGER is ducked down out of sight behind his overturned table. EDDIE has rushed to the front of the stage. An unforgettable moment...

EDDIE   (*To audience*) Fuck the fuck off the lot of you!!!

He freezes with his fist raised. Everybody freezes except JEAN.

JEAN   We'll never open evenings again... (*To audience*) Poor Eddie and his American films... Happy endings with the good guy winning in a shoot out... in slow motion... He didn't know the Kelly Crew would fight dirty... Daft bugger. Don't tell the kids, but I loved that old Eddie. He never noticed me but that night – he was magnificent. That night my heart was singing to him...

(*sings*) *I know that love is blind*
But I am just invisible tonight
Though take me in your arms
And I know, I hope
One honey kiss will start
The fairground of your heart

ROGER rises from behind his overturned table and joins in with this song, singing it to JEAN unnoticed, while she is singing it to EDDIE.

JEAN   *Run*

JEAN / ROGER   *Runaway with me*

JEAN	*Kiss me*
ROGER	*On a steamship*
JEAN	*In a snowdrift*
ROGER	*On the wingtips*
JEAN	*Of an airplane*
ROGER	*In a tailspin*
JEAN / ROGER	*Falling…* *Through storm clouds* *Above the rolling seas*
JEAN	*And then* *In the morning* *We'll do it all* *again*
JEAN	(*to audience*) I've got over it now. I've got two cats and I bake cakes.
PJ	Didn't they go round the back and kill Eddie's dog?
JEAN	Vanished it. Kidnapped it. Eddie must have walked 20 miles –
EDDIE	(*unfreezes. To an audience member*) You haven't seen him have you? He's brown with a little furry… (*draws out a tail shape but freezes again with fist clenched*)
JEAN	Then at dawn… a noise at the door…

CHANTAL howls and runs to JEAN who holds her and covers her eyes.

The bastards had cut off his tail. And little Chantal, she's been running this place ever since -

CHANTAL I'm just putting the bins out...

CHANTAL exits.

JEAN So no, love – they didn't kill Eddie's dog. They came back and killed Eddie.

PJ Who's that then?

JEAN That ain't Eddie.

EDDIE (*his fist turns into a nervous wave. To audience*) You see that man I was just talking to. You didn't see him. OK? (*To PJ.*) That fellah who just left – you didn't see him. OK?

PJ (*PJ is holding a business card*) You mean Mr Higgins - Immigration Officer?

EDDIE What did you tell him, blabbermouth?

PJ Nuffin. I told him to speak to you.

EDDIE (*to audience*) He didn't mention Marika by name – just making inquiries... Was I aware of the law? The penalties?! (*To PJ*) And not a word to Chantal, you...

(*MARIKA is passing*) Marika, love – how do you think the trial period is going?

MARIKA I am brilliant - the best waitress you will ever have. On the other hand, the food is

51

disgusting. PJ can't cook. Your daughter sulks. Jean is past her best.

JEAN   (*pops up*) I heard that. (*Pops down*)

EDDIE   Listen, I want to offer you the job. Properly. Full-time. I shouldn't let you work for nothing. Bring your papers in tomorrow.

MARIKA   You can't wait 2 weeks?

EDDIE   We should make it official, legal – bring your papers in tomorrow.

MARIKA   Not until you give me the manageress position.

EDDIE   Chantal would do her nut, she'd go bonkers... Let's just put you on the payroll first.

MARIKA   I think about it. But pay me something cash now - just till the two weeks is up, yeah. My friend's bringing my papers next week.

EDDIE   I'm not sure I can pay you cash...

MARIKA   (*seductive*) You can, Eddie. How many burgers have you sold today? How many coffees? Nobody knows. It's all cash. It's between you and me.

EDDIE counts out some money from a wad. MARIKA takes the money and abruptly walks away.

EDDIE   You bring your papers in.

52

MARIKA	(*sweetly*) She's coming next Saturday. Just give me the time.
EDDIE	(*to audience*) Time? I keep waking up - all alone with me acid indigestion and I can hear every clock in Birmingham ticking ticking in the dark. Time is life, isn't it − and I can hear it gurgling down every plughole in the city...

Enter PJ.

PJ	Here's your fags, Eddie, and your change. And your *Cosmopolitan*.

He hands over a bag which Eddie quickly hides under the counter.

EDDIE	Ta.
PJ	I need to talk to you about Marika, about the money.
EDDIE	Let's hear it then.
PJ	Promise you won't give me a bollocking -
EDDIE	Spit it out.
PJ	Well, Marika is... I don't think it's right... that you don't pay her.
EDDIE	Oh... you think I'm a mean miserable miserly bastard.
PJ	No, no... it's just if you don't pay somebody... they could be tempted to steal... Or something.

EDDIE   Are you trying to tell me she's a thieving little cow?

PJ   No, no... it's just how can she survive?

EDDIE   You're too late. I am paying her. Not that it's any of your effin business.

PJ   (*to audience*) Oh... There's just one good thing about today... I am now... officially... on holiday! (*rips off his tearaway chef's trousers*)

The lights go low. PJ tows a suitcase for the rest of the scene.

               (*lowers his voice, yawning*) Mind you, if you want the cheap flights, you do have to go in the middle of the night –

The sound of frantic muted knocking on the shop door.

MARIKA   (*off*) Let me in, let me in!

PJ   But that didn't sound like the taxi.

MARIKA   (*off*) Let me in, let me in!

PJ hurries off to the door. Enter MARIKA, distressed.

MARIKA   Lock the door, PJ, lock the door. Turn the lights down... (*She does it herself*) Come away from the window...

MARIKA hides behind a chair in the darkness - terrified. PJ remains centre stage, fairly brave...

PJ   What's going on? What are you doing out?

MARIKA   Shopping.

PJ	It's 2 o'clock in the morning!
MARIKA	With the Kelly Crew
PJ	Oh, Christ... It's not drugs, is it?
MARIKA	No. It's just somebody... I don't think he followed me.
PJ	The Kelly Crew?
MARIKA	(*looking out*) Worse than that.
PJ	Nobody's worse than that... I'll ring the police
MARIKA	Yes, ring the police, get me killed, chopped up in little pieces... Oh, PJ, I need a friend. I need help. Listen, if they kill me I want you to tell my grandmother...
PJ	If you don't tell me what's going on, I will ring the police.
MARIKA	Swear on your life you don't tell anyone. Swear on Chantal's life.
PJ	I swear on... Eddie's life.
MARIKA	I'm not from Poland, PJ. I'm an illegal alien.
PJ	I knew it. The moon or Mars? I bet you're from a faraway galaxy a long time ago -
MARIKA	They are looking for me... the people who smuggled me into the country...
PJ	I knew you were on the run.

MARIKA   Have you got a gun?

PJ   Fuck sake, Marika. I don't shoot people.
            I'm a chef. I just poison them

MARIKA   I don't think he followed me... He would
            kick down the door by now.

PJ   And killed you?

MARIKA   Probably. But he'd definitely kill you.
            There he is!!!

*She points. Freaked, PJ dives for cover, knocking tables
everywhere.*

PJ   You create a diversion - and I'll cook him
            a dodgy sausage.

MARIKA stands up and peers at a member of the audience.

MARIKA   It's OK. It's not him. Sorry. I'm paranoid.
            He couldn't possibly find me here...
            Promise, PJ, not a word – to anybody...
            OK? I need a hug...

PJ   *You* need a hug? What about me? I need a
            hug.

They hug. Enter CHANTAL in dressing gown. Lights up!

CHANTAL   (*to audience*) Got 'em! Red-handed...

*MARIKA walks out. The lights get redder and redder during
the following argument.*

PJ   (*to CHANTAL*) We were just talking – she
            was a bit upset.

CHANTAL	I'll show you what fucking upset is. Talking about what?
PJ	I can't tell you. I promised her.
CHANTAL	You promised her?
PJ	Come on, Chantal...We are going on holiday...
CHANTAL	*We* aren't going anywhere. *You* go where you like.
PJ	We've got the tickets.
CHANTAL	Take lover-girl.
PJ	Don't be stupid.
CHANTAL	Go on your own then. I could do with a break from you – that'd be a proper holiday.
PJ	I will. I'll probably have more fun.
CHANTAL	Go on, then... I want you to.
PJ	I am, I'm going. (*He doesn't move*)
CHANTAL	You wouldn't dare...
ROGER	Taxi for Tenerife!

ROGER scoops up PJ in a wheely-chair and pushes him towards the exit while the rest of the cast sing and dance like devils. PJ has his case on his knees.

PJ	(*sings*) *Sat in the back of a black taxi cab*
	Hairy hands have grabbed the steering wheel
	But you're the crazy crazy reason

57

Why I'm driven by my demons
Let's

PJ/CHANTAL go to hell!!!!

PJ   *Oh devil driver keep grinnin*
            Take me to the drink and the women
            Let's go to hell!!!

ALL   *You're the crazy crazy reason*
            Why I'm driven by my demons
            You're the crazy crazy reason
            Why I'm driven by my demons
            Let's

CHANTAL   *go to hell*

ROGER   Tenerife actually.

*PJ points ahead as ROGER pushes him off. CHANTAL is
left alone.*

CHANTAL   (*sings sadly*) *How I miss your candy kisses
            babe*
            *How I wish the memory would never fade...
            away*
            Tell me how you need me
            Don't walk away
            Never leave me
            How I miss your candy kisses babe...

            Oh how will he cope without me...?

JEAN has entered.

JEAN   He's probably sitting on the balcony now,
            tears dripping into his Malibu, listening to

58

the soft twang of bikini thongs as the beach volleyball reaches a climax.

CHANTAL   I've been too hard, haven't I? ...But if I had a proper boyfriend, he would have stood up for me.

JEAN   Johnny From Mars – that's who you need. (*To audience*) That's what my mom used to call him. Johnny From Mars – (*to a female*) that fabulous, perfect man you'd be with – if only you weren't stuck with your current twerp.

Enter EDDIE pulling on a clean white overall coat.

EDDIE   (*to CHANTAL*) You working – or you on holiday?

JEAN   Leave her alone, Eddie.

EDDIE   Sorry... I just wanted someone to put this sign in the window.

               OPEN TILL 10PM FROM SATURDAY.

CHANTAL   Christ, dad – you could tell me before we open in the evenings again.

EDDIE   I'm telling you now.

CHANTAL   Fuck's sake – we'll need more staff.

JEAN   I can only work till 9. The last bus goes at-

EDDIE   Marika's friend's coming.

CHANTAL   Oh, Marika's friend's coming! Is that it? Is that all the bad news?

JEAN tiptoes away from the battlezone.

EDDIE   And we're going vegetarian. Look, you've
               always said this place needed to be
               different. And that's it – a vegetarian
               Roller Diner – open evenings!

CHANTAL   Dad, she's gotta go - Marika - tell her to
               leave... Dad! Dad!

*She follows EDDIE off – almost bumping into MARIKA
carrying her coat.*

JEAN   (*to MARIKA*) I hope you are proud of
               yourself, young lady – upsetting Chantal?

MARIKA   I'm always proud of myself. (*Pause*) I
               think you don't like Polish people.

JEAN   It's not personal, love, I like Polish people
               in *Poland*. But we've just got too many
               here. It's getting a bit crowded now, a bit
               squashed... Still, you'll all be gone soon.

MARIKA   Oh, I see... you go on that march next
               week – with your big boots, waving your
               flag... I've seen the posters.

JEAN   I don't go on demonstrations, love.

Enter EDDIE and ROGER from opposite directions.

EDDIE   Black and Decker

ROGER   Workmate.

EDDIE is looking under the counter.

JEAN   You think England's a cushy number – all
               mermaids in the canals – angels working in

the Roller Diners. But it's not like that is
it, Eddie?

*He's found what he's been looking for - the bag with the
Cosmopolitan in it. He hides it behind his back.*

EDDIE   What? England...? It's like America,
               innit... But not so good. Yeah.

He exits

MARIKA   I tell you what England is. England is
               freedom. It is kindness. England is
               beautiful pop songs. And I'm not going to
               let the English spoil it for me. You? How
               many years? You don't even try to roller
               skate.

She goes to leave the shop.

JEAN   Hang on, hang on. You listen to me,
               Marika, in the end there are only two sorts
               of immigrant – good immigrants and bad
               immigrants. That's the only thing that
               matters – which sort are you? ...Just
               something to think about.

MARIKA   I am good immigrant. (*She beams and goes
               to leave*) What sort are you?

JEAN   What?

MARIKA   Just something to think about.

JEAN   We were here first, you cheeky madam!
               And before that we were part of the
               Empire.

MARIKA   Exactly, you are yesterday, I am tomorrow. And P.S. – your man is staring deeply, deeply in love with your bottom.

ROGER looks at the ceiling as JEAN spins around. MARIKA has gone.

JEAN   Somebody tell him...

                (*sings wearily to audience*) *I ain't loving any more*
                My heart is worn
                I've seen it all before

                I ain't feeling dizzy
                I ain't getting sweaty
                I ain't squeezing anybody's body anymore...

                (*spoken*) Not after 20 years hoping Eddie would notice me... I get on with my own life now... me and me cats,

ROGER   (*sings but JEAN can't hear*) *But I*
                Got loving I can sing for you
                I... got loving that can light your gloom
                I.... –

JEAN   (*still to audience*) *– ain't loving any more*

ALL   (*sing*) *...ain't loving any more*

ROGER can't speak to her as she takes a cup from his table and sashays back to vanish behind the counter. CHANTAL enters backwards... still arguing with the offstage Eddie.

CHANTAL   Well, somebody should tell her... if you
               can't, I will. (*Her fire drains away*) Oh,
               PJ...

               Don't walk away
               Never leave me

*PJ has entered quietly, tip-toeing towards CHANTAL and
gently joining in with the last line until they are in love...*

CHANTAL/PJ   *How I miss your candy kisses babe...*

ALL   *Ber wuh Ber wuh Ber wuh*
               Ber whu whu –

CHANTAL   You bastard! How could you piggin leave
               me? How could you go without me?

PJ   (*soothing*) I haven't been anywhere. I've
               only been to Gatwick – and back... on the
               coach...

CHANTAL   Have you?

               (*She melts...*)

PJ   Yeah... I couldn't go without you, could
               I? It was only when I got to the airport
               that I realised... my passport's in your
               handbag.

CHANTAL   Twat!!!

               (*She storms off.*)

PJ   (*to audience*) Fucking hell... I only wanted
               to go to Tenerife cos Toe-Jam went there
               for his honeymoon – a couple of months

ago, spent the whole time bonking his brains out... Toe-Jam never has these problems. His stag weekend in Brighton – best weekend of my life – except Chantal wasn't there. Shall I tell you how I know it was the best weekend of my life? Can't remember a thing! Must have been brilliant. Me, I just screw up. Sometimes, I wish there was someone older and wiser to tell me what to do...

JEAN has entered and holds her hand up. She hurries forward.

JEAN   (*sings*) *Under rising moons*
                  Lonely girls
                  Sing like Adele
                  In pink bedrooms

                  Curtains close
                  Against the stars
                  Lonely girls
                  In suburban homes are
                  Wild at heart

                  But when a girl becomes a woman

ALL   *uh oh*

JEAN   *When a girl becomes a woman*

ALL   *uh oh*

JEAN   *She doesn't need a boy, doesn't need a man*
                  When a girl becomes a woman, she needs a hero
                  When a girl becomes a woman, she needs a...

64

ALL   *hero-o-o-o-*

PJ pulls his shirt open to reveal a Superman T-shirt. He stands with his arms aloft, legs astride. CHANTAL suddenly races across the room and slams into his rock hard body and holds him fiercely. EDDIE and ROGER who have wisely been helping with the chorus have placed chairs next to each other so that the lovers can sit down as if on a sofa.

PJ   (*cuddly*) Been thinking...

> *Let's get a room together*
> *Full of happy feelings*
> *Maybe a bed of feathers*
> *Beneath a starry ceiling*

PJ/ CHANTAL *Cos we know that life is good*
> *On our sofa of love*

CHANTAL   *All we need*
> *For a happy day*

PJ   *za colour TV*

~~CHANTAL   *And a takeaway*~~

PJ   *All we need*
> *For a perfect night*

CHANTAL   *za Hollywood film*

PJ   *From a satellite*

PJ/ CHANTAL *On our sofa of love*

CHANTAL   *We could race around the town*

PJ   *Chase a million lovers*

CHANTAL   *But if we close our eyes, reach out*

65

PJ/ CHANTAL *We will find each other*
Cos we know that life is good
On our sofa of love

(*PJ starts to get out the wedding ring*)

CHANTAL Except now... you keep dirty little secrets from me... You and Marika.

PJ I gave her my word... She trusts me.

CHANTAL Well, now you can trust me too – or you can go on another holiday to Gatwick.

PJ But you've gotta promise, Chantal –

CHANTAL (*sweetly*) Or Heathrow – that's very nice at this time of the year...

PJ Christ... (*agonised*) She's an illegal immigrant –

CHANTAL Yes! Got her, got her, got her! I knew it, I knew it – and I found this in your pocket (*the business card*). Mr Higgins – Immigration! Go on, ring him up.

PJ I don't want to get her into trouble -

CHANTAL What about the trouble she's causing us? The cafe's going vegetarian.

PJ But that's what you've always wanted. I thought you'd be pleased?

CHANTAL I am – but my dad's only doing it because of her... Oh, I knew you wouldn't have the balls. (*She pulls out her phone to dial the number.*)

PJ	Hang on. Hang on. Look, I'll get her to leave, honest. We don't have to involve the authorities, don't even have to involve your dad - nothing. She won't want trouble. She'll leave, I promise. I'll just have a quiet word.
CHANTAL	Can I listen?
PJ	No... I'll choose my moment. (*to Roger*) Cos there's moments in your life, Rog — when you've just got to raise the roof,
ROGER	Lower the floor?
PJ	Shatter the windows
ROGER	Blow off the doors?

PJ sets a chair for MARIKA and invites her to sit down as dramatic sound builds up and stops -

PJ	So that's why you've got to leave, Marika. I want to marry Chantal... and I can't stand by while you are robbing the family... We are honest people, decent. I don't want to tell Eddie... but he'll find out in any case. Then he'll kill you — and if I haven't told him, he'll kill me as well.
MARIKA	You know a lot about men, do you? A lot about Eddie?
PJ	And you're causing trouble between Chantal and me. So until you leave I'd prefer it if you weren't so *friendly* with me.

67

MARIKA	I thought you were my friend. You haven't told her about -?
PJ	No, no... She thinks you are too familiar with me. As if you knew me.
MARIKA	I do know you... We met before... I've dyed my hair.
PJ	What? Are you some sort of stalker?
MARIKA	Oh, you think I want to sleep with you?
PJ	No...
MARIKA	Well, I have slept with you, PJ. And if we are decent people, we should tell Chantal.
PJ	You think Chantal is going to believe that? Shall I call her?
MARIKA	She'll believe it the way I tell her... She'll know it's true.
PJ	You crazy psycho bitch bunny boiler. This is England! You can't just make up lies...
MARIKA	Do you remember a seaside town – about 2 months ago – above a row of shops... in the flats, a little brothel?
PJ	(*puts his head in his hands*) Toe-Jam's stag weekend...
MARIKA	Lots of decent, honest Englishmen men on stag weekends, football teams on tour, family men. They all want to fuck me. You said...

PJ	(*drunk*) I want to fuck her. That one! (*sober, absolutely panicked*) Sssh!
MARIKA	You said I was
PJ	(*drunk*) the most beautiful woman I've ever seen. Ever. And foreign girls are dirtier, aren't they?
MARIKA	Are they? Shall we ask (*calling*) Chantal?
PJ	(*sober*) SSshh... Keep your voice down, please. I don't remember anything.
MARIKA	I know. I was just a bit of fun.
PJ	(*drunk*) Just pull your skirt up – then sit on that chair with your legs open. (*sober*) Stop it. I've never done anything like that before. I promise. I don't remember anything.
MARIKA	That's all right because I remember it all. You were sick on my shoes.
PJ	Oh God.
MARIKA	There is no God, PJ. There is just the devil, the devil... and us.
PJ	(*despairs*) This is some blackmail racket, isn't it? I bet you record everything –
MARIKA	I came into this country hiding in the back of a fruit lorry. I'm supposed to work in that stinking brothel to pay them back.
PJ	(*panicked*) What are you doing here then?

MARIKA   Do you know what they do to girls who run away? They shoot them – or give them a drug overdose. Vanish them. Probably into those burgers (*she makes a chopping motion*). So I vanish myself... new hair, new town, and my friend is bringing my new papers on Saturday.

PJ   Why here? (*drunk*) Just bring your skates – and I'll give you a job. You can count on me. (*sober, he is horrified by what he has just said*)

MARIKA   Roller Diner... the perfect heart of England. You told me all about Chantal and Eddie. And it was the only name I could remember – apart from the Tinsel Town Turbos – from Wigan.

PJ   What?

MARIKA   Football team I had to fuck. Oh, don't look so shocked – they were only seven-a-side... You are so honest, so decent – so you can tell Eddie, tell Chantal – or you can marry her. You never know, I probably end up as your mother-in-law.

JEAN enters. PJ flees.

JEAN   (*to audience*) I heard that... Well, the last bit.

Enter EDDIE.

EDDIE   Heard what?

JEAN	A word of warning, Eddie... This cafe is Chantal's sole inheritance.
EDDIE	What?
JEAN	If somebody much younger wanted to marry you, it wouldn't be for your body, would it? Or your sexy dance moves? It'd be for half of this place, wouldn't it?
EDDIE	Aaah... (*to audience*) And that's the price, I thought, for a wife like... Marika?
MARIKA	(*drying her eyes*) Not now, Eddie, honestly...
EDDIE	I just wanted to say if you are thinking of staying longer, making this your home, well, I'm not the sort of brute that some men are. I can be quite... *tender.*
MARIKA	Sexually?
EDDIE	I didn't mean it like that – but if you ever did want to be more than just a manageress...
MARIKA	(*laughs*) You are making me a proper proposition, Mr Business Brains Costello... a business proposition. It's taken you only 10 days to work me out.
EDDIE	Well –
MARIKA	It's so sweet of you, Eddie. Stand still, go on, close your eyes... Both of them.

He does so, leaning forward with puckered lips. She slaps his face as hard as possible and exits.

71

ALL   (*growing louder*) *How naughty how naughty how naughty how naughty*
                   How naughty how naughty how naughty how naughty

ROGER   (*reading Cosmopolitan*) "Sex is the tide, the flow, the undercurrent, the undertow to our world... we all Dance... *The Libido...*"

ALL   *Dance the libido*
                   Humpherharder humpherharder
                   Dance the libido
                   Humpherharder humpherharder

CHANTAL   (*into her phone*) Extension 432 – immigration department. Yes, Mr Higgins, please.

But PJ interrupts her and she hurriedly puts her phone away...

ALL   *Dance the libido*
                   Humpherharder humpherharder
                   Dance the libido
                   Humpherharder humpherharder

PJ   (*into his phone*) Extension 432 – immigration department. Yes, Mr Higgins, please.

But EDDIE interrupts him and he hurriedly puts his phone away...

ALL   *Dance the libido*
                   Humpherharder humpherharder
                   Dance the libido
                   Humpherharder humpherharder

MYSTERIOUS WOMAN and MYSTERIOUS MAN enter and dance oddly to their stations until they stand motionless either side of the stage holding their suitcases but still singing. MARIKA wearing her coat has appeared at a back corner of the stage as a silent brooding presence.

ALL   *Dance the libido*
                    Humpherharder humpherharder
                    Dance the libido
                    Humpherharder humpherharder

EDDIE   *(into his phone)* Yes, extension 432 - immigration department. Yes, Mr Higgins, please...

But CHANTAL interrupts him and he hurriedly puts his phone away...

ALL   *Humpherharder humpherharder*
                    (softly orgasmic) Ah!

End of Act 1

Act 2

No set change. Twilit stage. Marika in her coat with her suitcase. Other cast members are in shadow around the edge of the stage...

MARIKA   (*sings*) *2am*
           the wind is blowing
           The rain falls
           the tide is flowing

ALL   *The night belongs today*
           To runaways
           Ye-eh- eh-eh runaways

PJ   Chantal thought it was me - thought I was
           a hero because Marika had vanished.

MARIKA   *The skies are darkeni-ing*
           Horizon's closing i-in

ALL   *The only way you're gonna escape*
           Your yesterdays
           Is run run away

EDDIE   It was my fault, wasn't it? I mean
           underneath the toughness, she was still
           only a girl... delicate, fragile...

RADIO   *The night belongs today*
           To runaways
           Ye-eh- eh-eh runaways

EDDIE   I'd scared her away with my big fat
           hands...

Dawn... the Runaways chorus repeats as it fades away beneath the DJ...

RADIO   And if you are out on the streets today
             protesting, or protecting against the
             protestors protesting, wear your sun-tan
             cream! Is the heatwave going to end
             today – not until this evening! Wear your
             sun lotion! Slap it on your bald patch, slap
             it your nose, slap it on your belly while
             you listen to this timeless classic from
             yesteryear –

EDDIE kills the radio stops as the lights come up full in the
café and CHANTAL pops up and starts her song instantly.
She is behind the counter, chopping... MARIKA and PJ are
gone. MYSTERIOUS WOMAN and MYSTERIOUS
MAN are at their tables at the front of the stage.

CHANTAL   (*sings*) *Chip chip chip chip*
               Happy chappie
               Chuck chuck chuck chuck

M.MAN/M.WOMAN   (*join in*) *Chuckle girl.*

CHANTAL   *Chop chop chop chop*

M.MAN/M.WOMAN   (*join in*) *Happy chippie*

CHANTAL   *A happy day*

M.MAN/M.WOMAN   (*join in*) *In a happy world.*

CHANTAL   *Chip chip –*

EDDIE   Do you have to be so bleedin cheerful?

CHANTAL   (*to audience*) Like a bear with a sore arse he
               was – since Marika went.

EDDIE   PJ hasn't heard from her then?

75

CHANTAL   Why would PJ hear from her?

EDDIE   I dunno... This would have been her last day... Where is he in any case?

CHANTAL   Post office. Changing his euros back into money.

EDDIE   Oh, we serve magic sausages now, do we? Sausages that cook themselves. What does he think this is – a bleedin holiday camp?

CHANTAL   (*to audience*) I was a bit disappointed she'd gone really – cos I've got the whole café rigged to catch her stealing – all the notes marked, every tea bag numbered... Magic sausages? A baked bean couldn't hop across that floor now without me knowing about it –

MARIKA has entered from the street... agitated.

           Ohh... for Chrissake!

CHANTAL, disappointed, exits into the back.

EDDIE   What time do you call this?

MARIKA   Sorry... Sorry o'clock.

EDDIE   We thought you'd left – buggered off back to your palace in Poland.

MARIKA   I had left, Eddie. I can't stand violence.

EDDIE   You hit me.

MARIKA   Well, I forgive you...

76

EDDIE   (*to audience*) You've got to admit she's amazing. Just thought you'd pop in for your last day...? Say ta-ra to PJ...?

MARIKA   Thing is, Eddie, I've been thinking... I don't want this to be my last day... I'm going to stay longer...

EDDIE   Are you now? Well, smacking the boss round the chops isn't usually the best way to apply for a job. Not in England.

MARIKA   I couldn't hurt you, Eddie, I know that. You are like a mountain. You could crush me in those arms.

EDDIE   Well... it's still common assault that is.

MARIKA   I've sat in the station for a day and a half – watching the railway trains go into tunnels, going to the ocean, to the moon... and I couldn't decide where to go. The whole world lay before me...

               (*sings*) *covered in stars*
               I couldn't decide:
               The sea or the skies?
               Until the dawn
               When I realised...
               I wanna be here with you

M.MAN / M.WOMAN   *Among friends*

MARIKA   *I wanna be here with you*

M.MAN / M.WOMAN   *Among friends*

77

CHANTAL   (*pops up with knife*) *Among friends* (*pops down*)

M.MAN / M.WOMAN   *Among friends*

MARIKA   with you, PJ, Jean… You all need me. And my friend is arriving tonight for the gala opening. You'll like her, Eddie, she's a wonderful person.

> *I dreamed the stars*
> *I dreamed of the sea*
> *I followed moonbeams*
> *Until I saw*
> *Where I want to be…*
> *I wanna be here with you*

M.MAN / M.WOMAN   *Among friends*

MARIKA   *I wanna be here with you*

M.MAN / M.WOMAN   *Among friends*

MARIKA   *I wanna be here with you*

M.MAN / M.WOMAN   *Among friends*

CHANTAL   (*pops up with meat cleaver*) *Among friends* (*pops down*)

M.MAN / M.WOMAN   *Among –*

MARIKA   So you were right, Eddie, and I was wrong… we get married.

EDDIE   What?

MARIKA   Not straight away. Next week. I'll have my papers. We'll make a wonderful team. Fantastic. We'll make this place the greatest Roller Diner on Planet Earth. I know – I don't love you Eddie, no. But I still give you the great sex, don't worry, upside down back to front.

EDDIE   Love is still a very important part of a –

MARIKA   Pah! People tell you they love you – they cover you in kisses – all over – they love your little piggy toes – 10 minutes later they love somebody else. We are talking business, Eddie, business business. If you need love, you need a stupid sort of woman. Like Jean. Jean loves you.

EDDIE   Jean's not a woman.

MARIKA   Exactly.

EDDIE   She's my best friend. Her and Rog.

MARIKA   And I don't think friends give you the best sex – but me, I don't even mind that you are a bit smelly.

EDDIE   I don't smell.

MARIKA   You *pong*. But don't worry, twice a week, I give you a bubblebath. Double bubbles on Sunday. Deal?

She holds out her hand to shake but CHANTAL enters.

EDDIE   Well, give Chantal a hand. Get your uniform on.

MARIKA   First... I eat something.

Exit MARIKA.

CHANTAL   Anyone else you would have sacked them.

EDDIE   Oh don't start.

CHANTAL   Two days off and then she just waltzes in –
             I swear she's robbing us.

EDDIE   You show me she's been stealing and I'll
             break her thieving little fingers in the door
             jamb.

CHANTAL starts to exit.

EDDIE   Where you going?

CHANTAL   Stock check.

EDDIE   You've never done a stock check before.

CHANTAL   Never had a thief working here before. Ask
             PJ if you want to know what she is.

EDDIE   I'm not asking PJ anything – Chantal! I'm
             not serving.

CHANTAL   Get Marika's friend then.

EDDIE   She's not coming until tonight – for the
             opening.

CHANTAL   And she's probably some thieving old
             slapper as well...

CHANTAL storms out again. Lights on M.WOMAN.

M.WOMAN   (*to audience*) I steal things, yes, but only
             to help my friend.

M.MAN   (*to audience*) Her friend... Do you know
             what we had to do when she ran away? We

had to close that brothel. Within an hour. Every trace. But still I want to wind my fingers in her hair and bend her backwards... until she breaks. Destroy her... before she destroys me...

M.WOMAN (*to audience*) And now the sky lies heavy upon us.

M.MAN And I know who helped her to escape. (*still looking at the audience he points at MYSTERIOUS WOMAN with two fingers like a gun.*)

M.WOMAN (*to audience*) I don't want her to have a life like mine. I've got her new papers. (*She stands up*).

ALL (*sinister whisper*) Ma-ri-ka!

MYSTERIOUS WOMAN starts to exit. MYSTERIOUS MAN stands up – his "gun" still pointing at her.

M.MAN Oh I knew she would move... And when she did... (*as she goes to leave, his "gun" is pointing directly at the back of her head... but he relaxes*) I followed.

She exits and he follows. Enter PJ.

EDDIE Where have you been?

PJ Changing me euros...

EDDIE Oh, we serve magic sausages now, do we?

PJ What? There was a queue. And then some mob tried to burn the post office down. There's a riot starting out there –

81

EDDIE	Have you ever thought about just being honest for once?
PJ	I am honest... honest.
EDDIE	Oh yeah, so if I ask you any question, you'll answer honestly?
PJ	(*wary*) Well, yeah... unless it's a trick.
EDDIE	Alright, so answer me this then... Do I smell?
PJ	Of course not... No.
EDDIE	What about... *pong*?
PJ	*Pong*? Well.... only when you stand next to the fryers... But that's only because you are a bit fat. And it is a heatwave...
EDDIE	If I were you, PJ, I'd stick to telling piggin lies!

Exit EDDIE to the back.

PJ	(*to audience*) Oh big hard man Eddie – Jean told me that after they chopped its tail off, he never took that dog for a walk in daylight again. Scared of people laughing at him - and his dog with no tail – waddling down the street, terrified of the Kelly Crew. Tell you what, I'm glad Marika's gone – and if it makes him miserable... good.

Enter MARIKA – heading straight for the till, in uniform but carrying her coat.

MARIKA   Hi PJ! (*She is stealing again.*)

PJ   I don't believe it!

MARIKA   It's my last time, PJ, I promise... I *swear* -
            on Eddie's life.

PJ   Christ... What do you need that's so
            important?

MARIKA   Bullets.

PJ   What for?

MARIKA   A gun... So I can shoot you if Chantal
            finds out.

PJ   Very funny... Look, I've got my holiday
            money here...

MARIKA   I borrow that too –

But CHANTAL enters before PJ can hand it over.

CHANTAL   Off out again? Back today? Or next week
            maybe?

MARIKA   I pick up some things – for tonight. The
            Gala Opening!

CHANTAL   (*sweetly*) No rush...

MARIKA exits. CHANTAL pounces on the till.

            Keep a lookout! I knew it! These notes
            were marked and there's loads missing.

PJ   We can't just accuse her.

CHANTAL   Of course we can't. We do a stock check, a
            till reading, get my dad, count the money,

look in her purse – and then we ring the Serious Pigging Crime Squad!

PJ   Chantal?

He follows her off. ROGER sits at a table. Enter EDDIE who is carrying a clear plastic sack containing white clothes.

EDDIE/ROGER   Monkey wrench

ROGER   3-0

EDDIE   Offside

ROGER   Turbo.

EDDIE   4 be 2.

ROGER/EDDIE   Tits...

They stop as JEAN enters. She turns to ROGER.

JEAN   I've told you before – park your taxi outside... (*shouts off*) Alright PJ?

PJ   (*off*) Alright Jean.

ROGER   (*to EDDIE*) I can't park it outside – there's a riot out there.

EDDIE   (*freaked*) Yer what?

ROGER   It's that demo – it's all kicking off. They are burning down the post office...

PJ   (*pokes his head in from offstage*) See. (*withdraws*)

EDDIE   It's not the Kelly Crew, is it? Oh Christ, we open evenings again –

ROGER   Calm down, calm. It's going to rain later.
               Your English rioter can only riot when the
               sun's shining. We are an indoor race. The
               first drop of rain and he's back on the soft
               furnishings watching *Ant and Dec* on the
               47 inch.

EDDIE   I dunno... It's easy for you, Rog.

*JEAN sits down on a table opposite ROGER without noticing
him. But ROGER sees her.*

EDDIE   There's nothing you really want. You
               don't have to take any risks. But I've got
               to get a grip. Change a few things round
               here... Cos there's times in your life, Rog,
               when you've just got to raise the roof,

ROGER   Lower the floor?

EDDIE   Shatter the windows

ROGER   Blow off the doors?

*Dramatic sound builds up as EDDIE hurries off with the
sack. JEAN sits doing nothing. The sound stops -*

ROGER   Jean....

JEAN   I'm busy. (*to audience, suspiciously*) It was
               the first time he'd ever said my name.

ROGER   (*to audience*) I'd murmured it a million
               times in my heart.

JEAN   (*to audience*) And he'd got that look in his
               eye...

85

New song starts seamlessly, as ROGER goes into seductive mode.

ALL   *Dumb dumb chick*
                     Dumb dumb chick

ROGER   You are hotter than the heatwave... and hot enough... *tsss* – to melt me...

JEAN   I'm hot enough to bake cakes, love, and that's all I'm interested in... and there's somebody else.

ROGER   For a woman like you, there always is... But he won't give you what I'll give you.

JEAN   Won't he?

ROGER   (*sings*) *I'll give you heaven*
                     Wrapped up in stars

JEAN   *You say lovely things*

ALL   *Oh... You say lovely things*

JEAN   Listen, I've got two cats and I don't need some hairy man with a fathead.

ROGER   But *I'll give you heaven*
                     A lovin heart

JEAN   *You say lovely things*

ALL   *Oh... You say lovely things*

ROGER   Jean... just look at my feathers and love me.

JEAN   Ohhhhhhh.... I can't. There's someone else.

ROGER   Well, as long as it's not

JEAN/ ROGER   Eddie.

Enter EDDIE in a very white uniform, white trousers and a white garrison cap, plus sneakers.

EDDIE   What do you think? Do I look like the old Eddie or what? I've had this out the back for years.

Enter CHANTAL with PJ in tow.

CHANTAL   Christ, Dad – what do you smell of? Have you been using my body lotion? Jean bought me that for Christmas.

EDDIE   Makes a change from burgers...

CHANTAL   Don't think I don't know who you are dressing up for...

EDDIE   Really? Well, actually, I have got a few things I'd like to say. Where's Marika?

PJ   Popped out.

EDDIE   Well, a good moment to let you all know that I am going to ask Marika to become... my manageress...

CHANTAL   What?

EDDIE   Furthermore that I am considering marrying again –

CHANTAL   Dad, she's taking you for a fool.

87

EDDIE   Careful, Chantal.

Enter MARIKA carrying some bags. CHANTAL points at her.

CHANTAL   She's robbing you blind. She's stealing from the till –

MARIKA   (*ignores her*) Eddie – you look fantastic! I said it would suit you! And what's that sexy smell?

JEAN   Woodland Mist.

MARIKA   It's perfect for a proper gala opening...

She releases balloons from under the counter and other places. She pulls streamers across the stage...

EDDIE   Chantal says you've been stealing from the till.

MARIKA   (*pause*) OK, it's true. I hoped nobody wouldn't see me. But close your eyes, everybody –

EDDIE   I'd rather not.

MARIKA   -and I'll show you what I've bought - da-dah!

MARIKA takes off her coat like a stripper. She has added a waistcoat with golden wings to her uniform.

               A Roller Angel! The evening uniform. It's cheap, it's simple. We learn to skate-

EDDIE   It's brilliant.

CHANTAL   Hang on, hang on...

MARIKA	I've got some for all the girls. We'll look fantastic…

She holds them out.

CHANTAL	I wouldn't be seen dead in those -
MARIKA	and a new hat for PJ.
CHANTAL	He doesn't wear hats. How much did all that come to?
MARIKA	Who knows?… 50 pounds.
EDDIE	That explains it then…
CHANTAL	Count the money, PJ.
MARIKA	And Eddie, I've bought you a dickey bow! You'll look so smart tonight.
JEAN	Eddie would never wear a dickey bow, love.
CHANTAL	I think that money is going to be short by a lot more than 50 quid.
MARIKA	(*offers the bag of waistcoats*) But these are presents for you…
CHANTAL	You can't buy people presents with their own money.

MARIKA pauses and then drops the bags on the floor.

	Sit down if you don't want us to call the police.
MARIKA	You don't call the police…
CHANTAL	Let's see how much you've stolen first.

MARIKA	Eddie, you tell her - she doesn't call the police.
CHANTAL	Is that because you are an illegal immigrant?
PJ	Chantal?
CHANTAL	PJ told me. Because he confides in me. We trust each other. That's what you need when you work with people. Trust.
PJ	Fuck's sake... Chantal.
CHANTAL	Count the money! He tells me everything.
MARIKA	OK... I tell everybody everything as well.
PJ	Oh fucking hell.
MARIKA	Eddie, I was smuggled into this country. But tonight my friend is bringing me some good papers. No-one will ever know they are not my papers. Tonight I am free to stay. No-one will ever investigate me.
CHANTAL	They'll investigate when they know you are a thief. PJ, how much money's in the till?
MARIKA	I needed to buy something, Eddie. To save my life... protect myself...
PJ	How much should there be...?
CHANTAL	Just say!
PJ	440 pounds 72 –

CHANTAL   What?! There should only be 230! How can there be more?

EDDIE   Well, there's no problem then, is there?

CHANTAL is checking the cash...

CHANTAL   PJ, what are you doing? You've put your holiday money in here.

PJ   I haven't.

CHANTAL   There's your receipt from the piggin Post Office... euros to pounds. Why are you covering up for this... whore?

PJ   Don't call her that...

CHANTAL   Why not? She was offering to give my dad a bubblebath earlier. Double bubbles on Sunday.

JEAN   Eddie?

EDDIE   Nothing was finalised.

CHANTAL grabs MARIKA's handbag.

MARIKA   You have no right to look in my bag.

CHANTAL   If you don't want me to phone the police, I do.

EDDIE   Chantal!

MARIKA   You promise me – if you look in that bag you don't call the police. You swear – on Eddie's life.

CHANTAL   I won't swear on anything. I'll show you how much she's stolen. (*She looks in the bag and puts it down very carefully.*) Jesus... Call the police.

EDDIE   What is it?

CHANTAL   It's a gun...

JEAN   Shit... See, this is what they bring with them, the new ones.

MARIKA   I bought it here. Off the Kelly Crew. If I'm staying, I need to protect myself -

CHANTAL   And now we've got her friend coming as well. Another thief and a whore.

JEAN   Who's next for a bubblebath?

ROGER half raises his hand... but thinks better of it.

MARIKA   (*stops. Icily*) You do not call my friend a whore.

CHANTAL   Oh, I see, I can call you a whore – but not her.

MARIKA   Yes, you call me a whore. But not my friend. You are not worthy to call her anything. You don't know anything...

CHANTAL   You are a whore.

JEAN I knew it.

MARIKA   Not any more, I am waitress – nearly manageress.

CHANTAL paces up and down. She's thinking, muttering to herself.

CHANTAL   Why was PJ putting his money in the till?

PJ   (*to audience*) She was a bloodhound...

JEAN   (*to audience*) Getting nearer with every sniff...

CHANTAL   How did she know all about us?

JEAN   (*to audience*) Imagine... a man you trust and love...

CHANTAL   My skin began to crawl.

JEAN   (*to audience*) visiting prostitutes...

CHANTAL   Dad?

EDDIE   Poppet?

CHANTAL   You disgust me...

EDDIE   What?

CHANTAL   (*to MARIKA*) It's my dad. He's one of your clients... double bubbles on Sunday. (*To EDDIE*) Making PJ cover up for you. That's why you don't mind her stealing –

EDDIE   Chantal!! (*Silence*) I haven't been to Brighton in my life.

CHANTAL   Brighton???

EDDIE   That's where she's from...

All eyes turn to PJ who stands paralysed.

93

PJ   Nothing.

He is slowly dropping down behind the counter.

CHANTAL   Oh god... Toe-Jam's stag weekend... Get
                out of my sight! Get out of my sight!!

*PJ scuttles off. To prevent murder, JEAN grabs
CHANTAL.*

CHANTAL   (*to EDDIE*) You see, that's who you were
                going to marry.

MARIKA   You can still marry me, Eddie. I don't
                want to go.

EDDIE   I don't think I should, Marika, love... I
                think I should probably marry Jean.

ROGER is devastated. JEAN is astonished.

                I didn't mean to say it like this... but
                Marika, well, you want somebody exciting,
                thrilling... I mean who'd want somebody
                like me? With me bad breath? Me in-
                growing toenails?

JEAN raises her hand sardonically –

MARIKA   But I still be manageress? We still have
                the gala opening –

She pulls a streamer and a solitary balloon floats up.

JEAN   You can't stay, love. You've got to go.

MARIKA   Why? I thought everyone would like and
                love me by now...

JEAN	Because Mr Higgins is coming at 8 o'clock…
MARIKA	Who the fuck is Mr Higgins?
ALL	Immigration…
JEAN	He's coming to the opening… to find you.
MARIKA	(*to Chantal*) You invited him? (*To Eddie*) You? I have the right to know…
JEAN	(*pause*) I did. (*To audience*) This should be Chantal's cafe, really… You were causing too much trouble –
MARIKA	(*angry*) I'm the troublemaker? Me? You think I come here to raise the devil in your kitchen? Make the dogs bark and children cry? You don't know!! You don't know…
	Near my village they caught a man who made shoes for witches. Two plough horses pulled him apart until a demon slithered out of his belly. And the priest tried to kill it with a pitchfork while it squealed and squealed and all the trees burst into flames, one by one – all along the valley and over the hill.
CHANTAL	You're loopy mental, you are.
EDDIE	Girls…
MARIKA	(*upset*) Ok, I go, I leave – but don't accuse me of raising hell. I taste the smoke, I smell it in my hair. I tell you all, if I raise anything…

95

(she sings brokenly, alone) I'll raise heaven

> *Here where I stand*
> *With my bare hands*
> *I'll lift up the sky...*
> *Make everything... fine.*

She runs into the back. JEAN looks at the audience as she overhears the next exchange...

ROGER   Eddie, just to say I'm leaving too.

EDDIE   Yeah, see you later, mate...

ROGER   No, I'm leaving forever... you've found the woman of your dreams but I've lost mine. But she was a wonderful creature.

EDDIE   A very exceptional woman

ROGER   She was delightful...

EDDIE   There's not many like Marika...

ROGER   It wasn't Marika... someone much more exceptional...

EDDIE   Blimey... can't imagine anyone more exceptional than Marika, can you, Jean?

JEAN is looking at the audience

JEAN   Not off the top of me head, no.

ROGER   I never will again. That's why I'm never coming back.

EDDIE   Leaving town?

ROGER   Further.

EDDIE   The country?

ROGER   The planet.

EDDIE   You are taking it very hard.

ROGER   My heart's like a badger... squashed on the
            M6. (*He points at the chair*) And that's not
            really a taxi.

EDDIE   We know – it's a wheely chair.

ROGER   Actually... it's an intergalactic starship
            cruiser.

EDDIE   What... the GTi?

ROGER   Turbo...

EDDIE   I thought it looked a bit different...

ROGER   I crash-landed here a few years ago. Been
            waiting for the parts... But now, it's time
            to go. Maybe Jupiter, maybe Saturn - or
            maybe my home planet....

JEAN /ROGER   (*without looking at each other*) Mars...

ROGER   Where I'm known by my strange Martian
            name...

JEAN   (*without looking at each other*) Johnny...

ROGER   from Mars...

*He is wheeled around and out on his wheely chair by EDDIE
while JEAN sings. It would be nice to have some smoke and
sparks.*

JEAN   (*sings*) *Johnny from Mars*
                I love you
                Always wanted a boy from the stars
                Johnny from Ma-ars
                Johnny from Mars

                Plug your rocket into my heart and
                Recharge…
                (*Dahda da dada da*)
                Then depart

                Cos you're gonna get out of town now
                Gonna leave me behind
                Standing on the gro-ound
                Gazing into the sky
                Oh Johnny…

                I can't teach you how to cry
                While you're blazing
                Through the night skies
                But if you ever look behind
                You will see my planet weeping
                Oh Johnny
                Johnny from Mars…

ROGER has gone. CHANTAL comes to the audience.

CHANTAL   (*sings*) *I don't know the kind of girl I might*
                have been
                Woh hoh had certain things turned out
                differently
                People around said I had my head in the
                clouds
                Are they happy now
                I've come down to the ground?

MARIKA enters from the back with her coat... JEAN and MARIKA offer sad harmonies...

> *Walk on by*
> *Nothing to see here*
> *Sad to say*
> *It's ju-u-u-ust*
> *an everyday*
> *death of a dreamer*
> *Eyes now open wide*
> *but blind with tears...*

MARIKA   Chantal?

CHANTAL   *Walk on by...*

MARIKA   Sit down - and I'll tell you what happened that night.

CHANTAL   I don't want to know.

MARIKA   He turned up... a stag party, business men. Who cares? He was very drunk.

The drunk PJ staggers in.

PJ   (*drunk*) Piiiiissed.

MARIKA   He chose -

PJ   (*drunk*) Her. That one. Foreign girls are -

CHANTAL   Do I need to know this?

MARIKA sits PJ on a chair facing the audience.

MARIKA   You do – because you are a cruel and stupid bitch. You need to know something about your man that you are too blind to

99

see for yourself. He came to my room –
and I started to undress...

CHANTAL   He wouldn't have done it if it wasn't for
women like you.

PJ   (*drunk*) Just sit on that chair... no, no –
actually - put your legs together. Keep
your clothes on... I mean, you are very
lovely... but I already have a lovely
girlfriend –

CHANTAL   You're a liar.

MARIKA   Am I? When I said I didn't want a
boyfriend like PJ, I was lying. I would
love very much a boyfriend like PJ.

PJ   (*drunk*) She's soooh clever but her dad
only loves his dog who's dead... so Chantal
runs the whole place because... she's sexy!

MARIKA   And imagine me... I needed a home, I
needed to be with people as wonderful as
you... Where would you go... when you
are alone in a seaside town at night with
the rain coming sideways? Bad men
hunting for you? I could have run
anywhere in the whole world. I chose here.
I came here to join your family... Perhaps
we would be best friends like sisters –

PJ   (*drunk*) She does a wicked Lisa off *The
Simpsons*.

MARIKA/ CHANTAL Shuttup!!!

MARIKA	Me, I'm a bad immigrant, I steal money from drunk men's wallets – but I know what men are like... I've had their mouths all over me, their tongues inside me... but PJ, he is kind.
PJ	(*drunk*) All I'm saying is – just bring your skates. I'll find you a job.
MARIKA	Sssh. Go to sleep... (*to CHANTAL*) OK, I leave... pack my bag but I come back for my papers – see the Grand Gala Opening. And then if Mr Higgins doesn't catch me, I run away again...

PJ is asleep. Enter EDDIE. Enter JEAN. MARIKA is at the door.

EDDIE	I'll get your papers for you.
MARIKA	No, I need to see my friend, give her a hug... my only friend.
EDDIE	Marika...? The Kelly Crew are out there.
MARIKA	Don't worry, Eddie, I won't hurt them.

She leaves. EDDIE gazes entranced after her. CHANTAL sits thinking...

EDDIE The two most extraordinary people I've known in my life, leaving... on the same day.

JEAN	She is coming back for the opening
EDDIE	Yeah... but then she's leaving again.
JEAN	At least you've still got me.

101

EDDIE   (*still gazing after Marika*) Oh, you'll always be here, Jean.

JEAN   (*hurting*) Fine... I think I'll go and freshen up before tonight.

EDDIE   (*still entranced*) Yeah, yeah of course. I'll be OK.

JEAN exits. EDDIE turns and exits snapping his fingers at PJ as he passes... PJ wakes up...

PJ   Has Marika gone? ...Did you speak to her?

CHANTAL   She told me everything...

PJ   Oh Christ... Well, you didn't believe her, did you? You know what she is... She's a thief, Chantal. She's a...

CHANTAL   What is she?

PJ   You know... she's a liar. Whatever she said, it's a lie. How can you believe that I would have acted like that?

CHANTAL   Like what?

PJ   Whatever she said. I mean, she knows you hate her. This is her chance to get her own back. Tell you a lot of filthy lies. Make you suffer. It's her revenge...

CHANTAL   I don't believe her. She's a liar and I don't believe a word of what she told me.

PJ   Thank God for that. Don't cry... I've rung the authorities, like you wanted...

102

CHANTAL	That is so sweet of you but you are too late. Jean has already reported her.
PJ	Well, he's coming – Mr Higgins.
CHANTAL	I don't want you to touch me or speak to me ever again... Just go!!

EDDIE pops up behind the counter. He's wearing the dickey bow.

EDDIE	Hold on! We've got our gala opening. We need a chef. He'll have to go afterwards.
CHANTAL	Fine.
EDDIE	(*to PJ*) Go for a walk, son. Come back in a bit...
PJ	There's a riot outside...
CHANTAL	It's safer than in here.

PJ leaves.

EDDIE	(*to audience*) The rain still hadn't come – and people were running from the riot – scrambling out of the drains, falling out of the sky – hiding in our doorway, their faces pressed against the glass like a nightmare.

People clamour to be let in. EDDIE is spooked, he's pacing

> I thought maybe the Kelly Crew were out there... coming to eat me – and my dog. (*People are crying for help*) Oh... I didn't know whether to just tell them to fuck the fuck off, the lot of them, or... oh sod it...

103

EDDIE lets them in... PJ, EDDIE, CHANTAL, MYSTERIOUS MAN and MYSTERIOUS WOMAN (but not MARIKA) flood in with lots of noise. CHANTAL is wearing the Roller Angel uniform with wings.

PJ   They poured in – just to get out of the riot. Never seen a gala opening like it.

MYSTERIOUS MAN and MYSTERIOUS WOMAN have taken their seats on opposite tables at the front of the stage. MARIKA enters wearing her coat and towing her suitcase... Silence.

PJ   (*to audience*) She looked like a waif.

CHANTAL   (*to audience*) A stray.

M.MAN/M.WOMAN (*sing*) *A runaway.*

PJ   (*to audience*) And now she did look like a girl who could provoke murder...

MYSTERIOUS MAN stands up.

CHANTAL   (*to audience*) Because there is only one way to end a story in a Roller Diner...

PJ   What? American style?

CHANTAL   A shoot out.

PJ   In slow motion? (*To audience*) Oh Christ... I hope I'm not an extra...

NB. THERE ARE NOW SIMULTANEOUS TIME ZONES TAKING PLACE. THE SHOOT-OUT SCENE IS IN SLOW MOTION... BUT IT EVENTUALLY TRANSFORMS INTO A SCENE A YEAR LATER.

ALL   (*in slow motion*) Ma – ree – ka!

Everybody is moving in slow motion. MYSTERIOUS MAN waves a gun. MARIKA is running in slow motion towards EDDIE...

MARIKA   (*slow motion talk*) Eddie!!

EDDIE   (*to audience*) Of all the places she could have run, she ran... to me...

M.MAN   (*to the audience*) That's just because he was the fattest. (*Slow motion talk*) Marika, come to me. Your flesh and breasts belong to me...

EDDIE   I didn't like the sound of this.

M.MAN   (*slow motion talk*) And nobody gets hurt.

PJ   (*slow motion talk*) Would you like a dodgy sausage?

MYSTERIOUS MAN remains frozen but the rest of the cast can move.

CHANTAL   Our whole lives passed in front of our eyes.

EDDIE   Including our futures... (*slow motion talk*) You stay where you are, Marika...

CHANTAL   (*to audience*) It was a year ago now... but I remember it as if it was today.

PJ   And even though Eddie died –

EDDIE   Sorry? What was that?

PJ   She still made me leave.

CHANTAL   I couldn't stand the sight of him, the touch of him... thinking about where his fingers had been – his face...

M.WOMAN   For the sky lies heavy upon us –

M.MAN   and the demons in the bellies of men all opened their eyes and they whispered -

M.MAN/M.WOMAN   (*sinister whisper*) Ma-ri-ka!!

EDDIE   (*slow motion talk*) You stay where you are, pet. (*To MYSTERIOUS MAN*) And you, sunshine, you can fuck the fuck off.

M.MAN   (*to audience*) You saw it yourself: he put his big plump body between me and my woman. My woman that I like to fuck. He looked like a fat merchant who shoots monkeys.

Thunderclap, lights flicker. He turns and calmly shoots EDDIE. EDDIE begins to crash slowly to the ground... CHANTAL begins to wail - single notes each held for as long as she can. She is falling towards EDDIE one arm outstretched, the other behind her. PJ grabs her wrist to stop her falling... and they remain in that tableau centre stage...

M.MAN   At least the rain had come to end the riot.

M.WOMAN   (*to audience*) I headed for the door – I wanted to go home. Partly the gun crime, partly the riots... (*thunderclap*) mostly the weather.

MYSTERIOUS MAN aims his gun at her head. Everybody freezes. MYSTERIOUS WOMAN closes her eyes expecting her execution. MARIKA walks forward, placing herself in the

line of fire, the barrel of the gun on her forehead, she forces
M.MAN to step backwards...

MARIKA   You won't shoot me. You love my neck,
                you love me – stretched and naked. You
                love me when I whisper dirty words.

He lowers the gun but then raises it again...

M.MAN   Bitch! Whore!

MARIKA runs from the stage. The MYSTERIOUS MAN
fires after her so that we don't know if she has been shot.

PJ   I couldn't tell if she'd been hit.

EDDIE   I have! I've been hit.

M.MAN   The Englishman is the most dangerous dog
                on planet earth – a mongrel that thinks he
                is a pedigree.

MYSTERIOUS MAN shoots him again. CHANTAL's
wail goes up...

EDDIE   That's so unfair.

M.MAN   (*to PJ*) And you, don't *ever* insult me again
                with your sausage.

MYSTERIOUS MAN runs from the stage after MARIKA.
PJ flinches as a shot is heard offstage – and again! From now
on nearly all the speeches are direct to the audience.

PJ   We waited. Then we heard someone
                coming in.

They recoil...

EDDIE   Mr Higgins?

107

PJ   Nah, he never showed up.

EDDIE   Scared of the riot probably.

ROGER   (*off*) Hello?

*Enter ROGER and JEAN from different directions – She is
wearing the Roller Angel uniform with wings.*

ROGER   (*to audience*) I was just passing Venus
              when I heard the gunshots...

EDDIE   Help!

JEAN/ROGER Eddie!!!!

*Arms outstretched on either side of the stage, they advance as if
they are going to comfort EDDIE. Instead they comfort each
other over EDDIE.*

EDDIE   Hang on, I'm not dead yet...

ROGER   She was devastated.

*JEAN is in ROGER's arms. She gives a thumbs-up to the
audience.*

EDDIE   What about me?

JEAN   Because of the riots, the ambulance
              couldn't get through.

Chantal's wail goes up a note.

EDDIE   Take me in the taxi then...

A mad medley of songs continues to the end.

ROGER   But the taxi had been set on fire... in the
              riot.

Chantal's wail goes up a note. EDDIE staggers to his feet. ROGER is pulling on a white coat.

EDDIE   Oh don't bother, I'll go on the bus...

JEAN   But by the time he got to hospital...

ROGER   Dead on arrival.

EDDIE   (*has staggered to the exit*) I'm not so bleedin surprised!!

Exit EDDIE. Released by PJ, CHANTAL falls to her knees where her dad had lain a moment before.

CHANTAL   Dad?

JEAN helps ROGER into a pair of chef's trousers... while PJ reluctantly leaves.

JEAN   Well, with Eddie gone – and PJ – (*ROGER waves farewell to him*) we needed a new chef. And I didn't fancy starting again on Mars...

CHANTAL   Oh, Dad...

               (*sings*) *I'll brush your hair to one side*
               And won't cry
               Won't cry
               For you are a man who died
               With no fear left burning inside
               It's just your time
               Your time

ALL   *Your time*

JEAN   (*to audience*) I was worried about Marika though...

ROGER   All I saw was the rain washing the blood
                 gurgling down the drain... But no sign of a
                 body... She'll be all right – tough girl.

JEAN   Maybe she's dead... A Roller Angel...

*Thunderclap. Enter MARIKA on skates in a gold Roller
Angel outfit. The cast hum Runaways angelically. She's
otherworldly...*

MARIKA   *The night belongs today*
                 To runaways
                 Ye-eh- eh-eh runaways

ROGER   But we only eat veggie burgers now. Just
                 in case she's been... (*makes a chopping
                 action*)

JEAN   No... she'll be in America –

ROGER   New York!

JEAN   Probably got a restaurant – a Roller Diner
                 called

MARIKA   *Marika's* – the lights shining in the
                 pavement!

CHANTAL   Exactly a year ago she vanished – the day
                 my dad died.

Enter PJ.

PJ   The day she kicked me out... She went to
                 college.

JEAN   Attagirl! Business studies!

CHANTAL   I tell you now, those lecturers know
                 nothing. Me and Marika – we could show

110

'em how to run a business. But at least I met some intelligent boys.

PJ howls like a werewolf – exactly mimicking the MYSTERIOUS MAN's howl in Act 1.

CHANTAL   I slept with two of them.

PJ   (*howls. Stop.*) I got a job at Burger King. No-one wants to sleeps with you if you work at Burger King. Oh, I missed this place... That's why I needed to be here today, to see Jean, Chantal... I just walked out of Burger King, down the street – pulling on my silly trousers –

CHANTAL   And in through that door... Standing there! I hated him – hated him.

She runs across the stage – but hugs him fiercely.

          How could you pigging leave me?

PJ   Maybe we'll get a room together...

CHANTAL   We are taking it slow of course...

PJ   Maybe a bed together... Perhaps one day a little –

CHANTAL   dog

PJ / CHANTAL   Together...

CHANTAL   Cos I do love his silly trousers.

PJ   I love her... (*CHANTAL glares*) – sweet nature.

JEAN   (*about ROGER*) I love his fat head.

111

ROGER	I love her fat arse.
ALL	(*sing*) *Ohhhhhh…. You say lovely things* *Ohhhhhh…. You say lovely things*

Instantly merges into LIFT UP THE SKY intro Tum diddy
tum tumtumtum…

ROGER	And we do need another chef… (*throws a chef's jacket to PJ*)
JEAN	Cos me hot cakes are selling like…
ROGER	Plus Eddie's murder…
JEAN	(*confidentially to audience*) Best advertising we ever had…
PJ	Dead Eddie's – Vegetarian Roller Diner –
CHANTAL	a little piece of heaven here in dirty Birmingham…
JEAN	Open evenings…
MARIKA	(*sings*) *I pray-ay* *For the day-ay* *When everything's fine*
ALL	(*joining in*) *everything's fine* *With mermaids* *In the river* *Floating by*
JEAN	and angels
ALL	*When everything's fine*
CHANTAL	It's a canal

MARIKA   It'll be a river by the time I've finished...

              Cos I'll raise heaven
              Here where I stand
              With my bare hands
              Count on me

(*CHANTAL and MARIKA bond on this line*)

ALL   *We'll raise heaven*
              And make it shine
              Feet on the ground
              Lift up the sky
              Make everything fine

EDDIE   (*off*) *Hear me* (*the cast listen bewildered*)
              When you're weary
              Hear me
              When you're lonely in the night...

Enter EDDIE on skates with Roller Angel wings and gold shorts.

              Hear me
              I want you near me

MARIKA   (*joins in*) *Hear me*
              I want you by my side when
              We lift up the sky

ROGER   (*sniffs the air...*) I think I can sense a presence...

JEAN   (*sniffs the air...*) Woodland Mist?

PJ   Or them sausages I burnt...

EDDIE   Charmin.

JEAN   But in a way this place is always haunted
              by…

MARIKA   Marika Malinksi!

CHANTAL   (*admiringly*) Superduper waitress!

JEAN   And Eddie…

EDDIE   (*American accent*) Who's asking?

MARIKA   Mr Business Brains Costello…

EDDIE   The ghost of the man I could have been.

SEVERALLY   *O I'll raise heaven*
              Here where I stand
              With my bare hands
              Count on me

              We'll raise heaven
              And make it shine
              Feet on the ground
              Lift up the sky
              Make everything –

EDDIE   (*to audience*) Fuck the fuck off, the lot of
              ya!

Blackout. The End

Polish My Boots

Candy Kisses

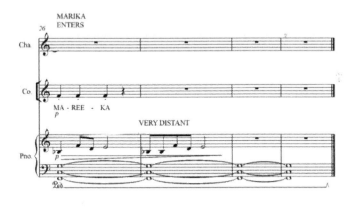

A Quiet Life

Stunning World

P.J. in my head, and in my heart, and my hearts in flames

Co. La-la-la-la

Pno. D/A E/A D/A E/A A

ff   mf

CUT OFF WITH CUE.
I've found it.

P.J. Stun-ning world stun-ning stun-ning

Co. la. Stun-ning world stun-ning stun-ning

Pno. D/A E/A D/A E/A

Choosin' Shoes

Rain On Your Back

Fairground Of Your Heart

Go To Hell

Candy Kisses (No.1 Reprise)

I Ain't Lovin' Anymore

When A Girl Becomes A Women

Sofa Of Love

Dance The Libido

REPEAT UNTIL CUE:
'Sex is the tide, the flow,
the undercurrent to our world...
we all Dance..The Libido...'

Runaways

Chuckle Girl

I Wanna Be Here With You

with you   I wan-na be here   with you   A-mong

A-mong friends   A-mong friends

CHANTAL

CUE: MARIKA

"With you, P.J. June. You all need me. And my friend is
arriving tonight for the gala opening.
You'll like her, Eddie, she's a wonderful person

friends

A-mong friends

FREELY

I dreamed the stars   I dreamed of the

3

CUE: MARIKA:
So you were right, Eddie, and
I was wrong...   we got married

You Say Lovely Things

Lift Up The Sky

Johnny From Mars

Death Of A Dreamer

to see here   sad to say   It's ju____st   an   eve-ry-day death of a
C#m/   A   B   C#m   C#/B

MARIKA:
Chantal?

dre-eam-er   Eyes now o-pen wide   but   blind with te-ars ...   walk on by...
C#m/   D/A   B   E

163

24. Polish/Runaway v5

24 The Sky Weeps (in E)

CUE: JEAN.
I was worried
about Marika

(Cast HUM)

Lift Up The Sky